ON THE SANTA FE TRAIL

JAMES A. CRUTCHFIELD

D1607603

TWODOT®

GUILFORD, CONNECTICUT
HELENA, MONTANA

A · T W O D O T® · B O O K
An imprint and registered trademark of The Rowman & Littlefield Publishing Group, Inc.
4501 Forbes Blvd., Ste. 200
Lanham, MD 20706
www.rowman.com

Distributed by NATIONAL BOOK NETWORK

British Library Cataloguing in Publication Information available

Library of Congress Cataloging-in-Publication Data available

ISBN 978-1-4930-3986-9 (paperback)
ISBN 978-1-4930-3987-6 (e-book)

∞™ The paper used in this publication meets the minimum requirements of American National Standard for Information Sciences—Permanence of Paper for Printed Library Materials, ANSI/ NISO Z39.48-1992.

Printed in the United States of America

*To the memory of Josiah Gregg,
who wrote the first comprehensive book
about the Santa Fe Trail.*

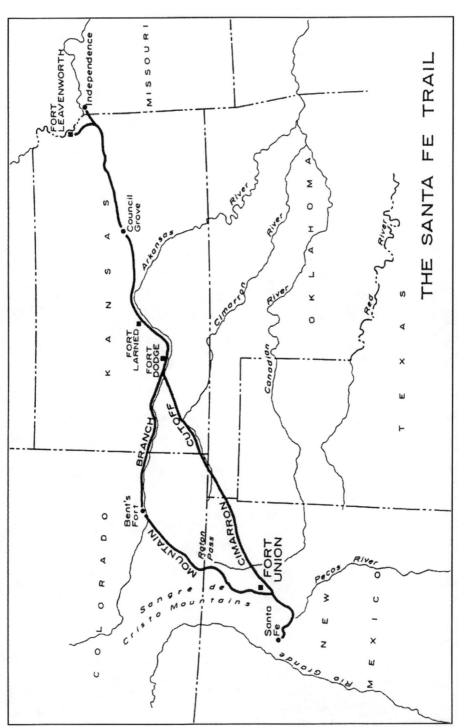

THE SANTA FE TRAIL

Map of the Santa Fe Trail. COURTESY OF JAMES A. CRUTCHFIELD

CONTENTS

CONTENTS

INTRODUCTION

YEARS AGO, BEFORE INTERSTATE HIGHWAYS CRISSCROSSED THE FACE OF the United States, travel from one point to another throughout this vast land was difficult indeed. Before the automobile and the airplane sped us to and from our destinations within hours, a person who needed to travel a mere twenty or thirty miles was in for an all-day or more experience.

For a very long time after the early colonists settled the eastern shoreline of the United States, even short travel between nearby colonies was arduous, and there were no routes to follow except the undeveloped trails that the Indians had made through the wilderness. In time, however, the settlers began thinking about how to improve these pathways so that travel between villages could be made easier. Before long, a system of roads stretched up and down the Atlantic coast connecting such towns as Boston, New York, Philadelphia, Baltimore, Charleston, and Savannah.

Little travel was done in the backcountry in those days, since nobody really knew what mysteries might lurk to the west of the thin stretch of settled land along the seaboard. Those few hardy adventurers and explorers who did fathom this pristine wilderness simply made their own trails through the thick forests, or else used one of the common Indian or animal paths.

By the time the Civil War arrived, most of the United States east of the Mississippi River was filling up rapidly with people, and the region had a pretty good network of roads that varied greatly in the degree of comfort they provided for travelers. The highways connecting the major cities were wide and relatively pleasant to travel, either on horseback or in a carriage or wagon. But the roads that existed in rural sections were crude, indeed, as they snaked their ways through forest and field. Narrow, rocky, and rough on a horse's hooves, these primitive pathways sometimes even completely washed out in wet weather.

In that vast region of land that lay beyond the Mississippi River, there were hardly any roads at all for a long time. After a while, though, a few thoroughfares sprang up here and there, linking towns and villages together in the more densely settled areas near the Mississippi. Still, only a handful of longer highways existed to transport emigrants and freight across the endless Great Plains and over the Rocky Mountains and beyond. In fact, as late as 1860, the majority of this huge region that stretched all the way to the Pacific Ocean, and from Canada to Mexico, was so sparsely populated that there was little justification for building roads.

The Santa Fe Trail was the oldest of these overland highways. It opened for American traffic in 1821, and although it was used until the coming of the railroads in the 1880s, its heaviest commercial usage occurred between the middle 1820s and the Civil War. The Trail extended from the American settlements located in westernmost Missouri to the Mexican town of Santa Fe in present-day New Mexico. Its path followed some of the wildest, most desolate—yet beautiful—country in America as it traversed today's states of Missouri, Kansas, Oklahoma, Colorado, and New Mexico.

In the pages that follow, the author has attempted to give a balanced history of the Santa Fe Trail. While he has relied on the works of many writers who have contributed to the vast literature of the trail, he takes responsibility for any errors of fact that may have crept in. Read on now about the life and times of the Santa Fe Trail and the people who traveled it during its long and useful life.

JAMES A. CRUTCHFIELD
FRANKLIN, TENNESSEE

CHAPTER ONE

Before the Santa Fe Trail Was a Trail

THE LAND THROUGH WHICH THE SANTA FE TRAIL WOULD ONE DAY RUN was originally occupied by several tribes of American Indians. Before there ever was a trail at all, numerous bands of tribesmen—first on foot, and later on horseback—roamed this particular part of the southern Great Plains in search of bison and other game. Other tribes practiced an agricultural lifestyle and inhabited sedentary villages.

Among the various tribes that an early explorer in the region would have met had he traveled from one end of the future trail to the other were, from east to west, the Kansa, Osage, Kiowa, Comanche, Cheyenne, Arapaho, Jicarilla Apache, and—when he drew near to the ancient town of Santa Fe itself—several groups of Pueblo Indians, who built their apartment-like buildings along the Rio Grande.

In the early 1700s, about one hundred years before the Santa Fe Trail opened up the lucrative markets of the Southwest to Missouri traders, the entire region had undergone a tremendous population upheaval among its indigenous inhabitants. Therefore, some of the tribes that lived and hunted in the vicinity of the Trail when it was first used by white traders had only recently arrived in the area themselves.

The primary reason for most of this mass movement of peoples was the pressure exerted by increased numbers of American settlers moving from the East toward and beyond the Mississippi River. As the new-comers relentlessly moved westward, they drove before them the various Indian tribes that they encountered in their migrations. These tribes, in turn, pushed the Indians in front of them ever westward, and so on.

Eventually, several tribes made long migrations just to get out of the way of the rapidly expanding frontier.

The Comanche, Kiowa, Cheyenne, Arapaho, and Jicarilla Apache were among the newly arrived tribes to take up residence along the future route of the Santa Fe Trail. They had originally lived north of the region—some near the headwaters of the Mississippi River, some amid the Bighorn Mountains of today's state of Wyoming, and some as far away as Canada. Members of these tribes were outstanding horsemen, and most were closely related to the bison-hunting culture that distinguished the Great Plains dwellers.

The Comanche, Kiowa, Cheyenne, and Arapaho lived in large tepees made from the hides of bison. These big, airy tents served as ideal homes year-round, remarkably warm in the winter and cool in the summer. No agriculture was practiced by these tribes, although some of them had farmed in their woodland villages back East. The Jicarilla Apache, poised on the border of the dry and hot desert Southwest, shared some of the traits of the bison hunters, but displayed differences as well. For example, since the bison's range barely touched the area in which this branch of the Apaches lived, its members were far less dependent on the animal as a means of livelihood. Consequently, their houses were made from grass, rather than bison hides, due to the relative scarcity of bison in their region.

Other local Indian tribes had been present for a long, long time when the Santa Fe Trail was first utilized for trade by Americans. The Kansa and the Osage in the East had occupied their lands for centuries and were, by and large, settled, agricultural people. They lived in spacious, mound-like, soil-covered homes, usually built high upon a bluff that overlooked a river or stream. Several of these houses made up a village, and the entire community was usually protected by a strong wooden stockade.

Both the Kansa and the Osage, in addition to living off the produce of their crops, supplemented their food sources by also hunting the mighty bison. Once a year, the inhabitants of the villages packed up supplies, weapons, and other necessary articles and moved out onto the prairie in search of the herds. Enough animals were usually killed during

Young Osage warriors. GEORGE CATLIN / PUBLIC DOMAIN

this one concentrated hunt to supply the inhabitants of a village with meat and hides until the following year's expedition.

Before the introduction of horses, which were brought into America by the Spaniards in the mid-1500s, all of the Indians who lived and hunted on the Great Plains either hauled their hunting and domestic gear themselves, or let their dogs drag it behind them on a travois, which was a carrying platform strapped to two long poles and fitted to the dog with a harness. The appearance and ready accessibility of horses, however, made a tremendous impact upon all of the native peoples of the Great Plains. Whereas before the horse arrived, a bison hunt required the efforts of everyone in the village, the same results, with horsepower, could be achieved much faster, far more easily, and with considerably less effort on everyone's part.

There is no doubt that the horse is the reason why so many of the tribes that inhabited the Great Plains rose to such heights in the arts of hunting and warfare. Horses allowed much greater distances to be covered in a lot less time. They also provided a means whereby the Indian hunter and warrior could get much closer to his prey than he could on foot. All things considered, it was the horse that literally made these Indians what they were—the lords of the Plains—by the time the first American explorers arrived.

At the extreme western edge of the territory through which the Santa Fe Trail would someday run lived the ancient Pueblo Indians. They had dwelled in their large, permanent, adobe apartment houses, called pueblos, for longer than anyone could remember, and pointed out with pride that they were the descendants of the original inhabitants of the region. Agricultural by nature, the Pueblo were noted for their fine pottery. The nomadic tribes from the East often traded with the Pueblo, swapping bison hides, meat, and other essential parts of the animal for agricultural produce. The most imposing reminder of Indian days along the Santa Fe Trail was the massive ruins of the pueblo at Pecos. This village was situated in the valley of the Pecos River in the shadow of New Mexico's Sangre de Cristo Mountains. The town was placed in a strategic location between other pueblo villages lying along the Rio

Grande to the west and the Great Plains to the east. Its location made it a natural stopping place for Plains tribes, such as the Comanche and Kiowa, who often visited the pueblo in great numbers to trade with the village's inhabitants.

As early as 1540, the Spanish chronicler Pedro de Castañeda described Pecos Pueblo, which at the time was home to at least two thousand people, as follows:

> *Cicuye [the Spanish name for Pecos] is a pueblo of as many as five hundred warriors. It is feared throughout that land. In plan it is squared, founded on a rock. In the center is a great patio or plaza with its kivas. The houses are all alike, of four stories. One can walk over the entire pueblo without there being a street to prevent it. . . . The houses have no doors at ground level. To climb . . . inside the pueblo they use ladders which can be drawn up; in this way they have access to the rooms. . . . The pueblo is surrounded by a low stone wall. Inside there is a spring from which they can draw water. The people of this pueblo pride themselves that no one has been able to subdue them, while they subdue what pueblos they will.[1]*

Another Spaniard, Gaspar Castaño de Sosa, described the clothing of the inhabitants of Pecos when he visited the pueblo in 1590.

> *The dress of the men, according to what we saw there—as it was the cold season—most or all of them wore a blanket of cotton and a buffalo hide over it. . . . The women [dress] with a blanket drawn in a knot at the shoulder and a sash the width of a palm at the waist. At one side, the blanket is completely open. Over it are placed some other very gaily worked blanket or some turkey feather robes and many other curious things.[2]*

In 1625 Spanish padres completed their first church at Pecos. Around 300,000 adobe bricks, each weighing forty pounds, were used in its construction. Some of the walls were twenty-two feet thick, and the church building itself had six different bell towers.

By 1680 Pueblo Indians all over New Mexico had grown tired of the Spanish yoke and attempted to drive the hated Europeans back to Mexico. They succeeded when a member of the Taos Pueblo named Popé organized warriors from most of the northern villages into a powerful force. The Pueblo Revolt, as the rebellion was called, pitted Indian against Spaniard, and when the insurrection was over, soldier and priest alike had been expelled from New Mexico.

Retreating to the area around today's El Paso, the disenfranchised Spanish could do little about their situation as they listened to endless rumors proclaiming that their one-time neighbors to the north had eliminated all vestiges of the Spanish presence in the region. Along with others, the beautiful church at Pecos was destroyed. A few years later, however, Spanish soldiers and priests reconquered New Mexico, and in 1717 a second church was completed on the site of the first building. Much smaller than the original church, the new sanctuary, nevertheless, served the needs of the Spanish who moved back to Pecos, as well as the Indian converts who worshipped there.

For years after the return of the Spanish, Pecos was a thriving place. The priests had introduced European farming technology, metal tools, horses, and wheat, and many of the village's inhabitants had converted to Christianity. Continuous warfare with the Comanche, however, along with European-introduced diseases, took their toll. By the 1770s, Pecos was no more than a vestige of what it had once been.

In 1838, after American traders began frequenting the Santa Fe Trail in great numbers, the last residents of Pecos, less than twenty individuals, moved to the pueblo of Jemez, thus leaving the magnificent ruins that can still be viewed today.

American Indians were not the only original inhabitants of the vast southern Great Plains. A rich diversity of wild animals called the region home as well. The most numerous large mammal was, no doubt, the bison. It has been estimated that as many as sixty million of the animals lived in North America at the time of its early exploration by Europeans. Bison were everywhere. The Spanish conquistadores were overwhelmed by the mile after endless mile of prairie and the countless thousands of bison that grazed upon it. Coronado reported:

> I reached some plains so vast that I did not find their limit anywhere that I went, although I traveled over them for more than 300 leagues. And I found such a quantity of cows [bison] . . . that it is impossible to number them, for while I was journeying through the plains, until I returned to where I first found them, there was not a day that I lost sight of them.[3]

Termed by the early Spanish as the "most monstrous thing in the way of animals that has ever been seen," the bison, more than any other animal,

An early Spanish artist's rendition of a bison. FRANCISCO LOPEZ DE GOMARA / PUBLIC DOMAIN

served as the Plains Indians' walking commissary, supplying them with practically 100 percent of the raw material they needed to survive. Josiah Gregg, a Santa Fe trader and author of a popular book about the Santa Fe Trail, recognized the dependence that the Plains tribes had on the great shaggy beast when he wrote, "This animal furnishes almost the exclusive food of the prairie Indians, as well as covering for the wigwams and most of their clothing; also their bedding, ropes, bags for their meat, etc.; sinews for bow-strings, for sewing moccasins, leggings, and the like."[4]

The speedy pronghorn antelope may have run the bison a close second when it came to numbers. As many as forty million of the fleet-footed animals may have called the Great Plains home during the early days of European exploration. Antelope hides made very fine leather, and the material was used for children's clothing, as well as for men's shirts and jackets. Some historic Indian tribes—the Cheyenne, for example—organized group antelope hunts that were held in much the same manner as bison hunts. George Bent, the son of Bent's Fort builder William Bent and his Cheyenne wife, Owl Woman, graphically described one of these hunts:

When all the men, women, and children had hidden themselves behind the lines of brush and the antelope priest was seated on the ground back of the pit with his medicine sticks in his hands, a few good runners were sent out on foot to drive the antelope toward the trap. When the antelope came running toward the pit, the priest kept singing to them and beckoning them forward with his medicine sticks until the whole herd rushed toward him and jumped into the pit. Sometimes there were so many animals that they could not get into the pit and some of them jumped over the ditch and came right where the priest was sitting; but he kept right on singing and beckoning with his sticks. If any of the antelope ran toward the brush lines to attempt to escape, the Indians hidden behind the brush yelled and drove the animals back. . . . When the trap was full of antelope, the priest gave the signal and the Indians entered and began killing the animals. . . . The animals were knocked on the head with clubs, and lariats were used to drag some of the animals out of the bottom of the pit.[5]

Wild horses were also common residents on the southern Great Plains. Descendants of the first horses brought to Mexico by Hernán Cortés, the mustangs had drifted farther and farther north with every passing year. It didn't take long for the Plains Indians, already used to traveling great distances on foot, to adopt the horse as a mode of transportation. After they became adept at riding, braves pursued the wild horses to add new blood to their own herds. George Bent wrote about how the animals were captured:

> Scouts were kept out ahead the same as in a buffalo hunt, and when they signaled that a herd of mustangs had been sighted, the hunters prepared to surround the herd. . . . The hunters moved up-wind to prevent the mustangs winding them, for if the wild herd scented the hunters it would be off instantly. Keeping behind the hills, the hunters advanced cautiously, and after coming as near to the herd as they could get, they began to spread out and make the surround. When everyone was in position the signal was given and a man mounted on a very fast horse rode out toward the mustangs. This man rode slowly, lying flat on his horse's back, until he was quite close; then he sat up and charged into the herd. This scattered the mustangs, which ran in every direction, but everywhere they turned Indians rode out from behind the hills and charged at them. Each hunter picked out the mustang he liked best and ran it down. Running the animals down was not very difficult, as these hunts were usually made in the early spring while the mustangs were still weak from a winter passed in a state of semi-starvation. Besides this, the animals were always full of grass and water and in poor shape for a hard run. Their wind was not good.[6]

Bent then described how the hunters tossed a noose over the mustang's head and "choked down" the creature until he stumbled and fell. A buffalo-leather halter was then slipped over the horse's head and he was tied up close behind a domesticated horse. A few days' association with the tame horses was usually enough to calm down the wild ones and make them approachable.

9

Other large mammals—deer, black bear, elk, Rocky Mountain sheep, and wolves—frequented the southern Great Plains as well. But, aside from the vast bison and mustang herds, the one animal that fascinated newcomers the most was the lowly prairie dog. "Of all the prairie animals, by far the most curious, and by no means the least celebrated, is the little prairie dog,"[7] wrote Josiah Gregg in his book, *Commerce of the Prairies*. Perhaps numbering in the billions and residing in towns that sometimes covered hundreds of square miles, the prairie dog was often described by early writers in almost human terms. The town had "streets" that seemed to be "paved," and observers reported seeing the communal rodents "cleaning house." But the little fellows were extremely hard to catch. "Attempts either to dig or drown them out of their holes have generally proved unsuccessful,"[8] lamented Gregg.

All in all, the land through which the Santa Fe Trail would one day pass was a province of rich natural and cultural diversity. Indians of one tribe or another had lived in the region for millennia, while others were recent arrivals themselves. But, regardless of whether the Native inhabitants were old or new to the area, all of them had become totally familiar and comfortable with their environment and had adapted to the land and the resources around them. All of this would change dramatically within a few short years, as American freight wagons began to roll through the tall prairie grass.

CHAPTER TWO

The Lure of Santa Fe

THE SANTA FE TRAIL ACHIEVED ITS GREATEST FAME DURING THE EARLY to mid-1800s as a road of commerce that linked Missouri traders with the rich markets of New Mexico. However, a curiosity existed in the minds of some Europeans and Americans that predated the actual commercial beginnings of the Trail. And, of course, there is no way of knowing just who might have used the Trail's later route during the years before regular trade was established with the people of Santa Fe.

It is believed that the first white man who made a trip across the Great Plains following the general path of the future Santa Fe Trail was not an American trader at all, but rather a Frenchman. Pedro Vial, whose real name was Pierre Vial, made the round-trip between Santa Fe and St. Louis in record-breaking time, considering the fact that his party was captured by Indians and held for six weeks during the first stage of his journey. The Frenchman set out from Santa Fe, which at the time was one of the northernmost settlements in New Spain, in May 1782, and reached St. Louis in early October. His return trip was begun in mid-June 1792, and ended in Santa Fe in mid-November. The commandant at St. Louis documented Vial's arrival there in a letter that he wrote to the governor at New Orleans:

> *Last night there arrived from the town of Santa Fe, in the kingdom of New Mexico, Pedro Vial and two young men who accompanied him. He was commissioned by the governor of that province . . . to open a road from that town to the establishments. . . . It appears that he will*

remain all winter in this place because it is not the season to undertake a return to Santa Fe. . . . I find myself obliged to supply them with the provisions and clothing that they will need during their sojourn, as well as the equipment necessary when they begin their [return] trip—all of which I shall do with due economy.[1]

But, even before Vial made his monumental trip across the southern Great Plains and back again, other Frenchmen had eyed the wealth of the remote villages of New Spain. As early as 1739, in fact, the brothers Paul and Pierre Mallet entered the sleepy town of Santa Fe after an overland trek that had carried them over parts of today's states of Missouri, Nebraska, Kansas, Colorado, and New Mexico. The Mallets lost all of their trading goods on the outward journey, and suspicious Spanish authorities, while treating the brothers well, detained them in Santa Fe for several months before allowing them to return to the eastern settlements. Two years later, the Mallet brothers attempted another passage to Santa Fe, this time via the Canadian River, but failed in their efforts.

Other travelers may have broken the silence and mystery of Santa Fe during the eighteenth century, but contacts with Spanish authorities there remained, for the most part, isolated. The Spanish were jealous of their possessions in northern New Spain, which in addition to today's states of Arizona and New Mexico, included parts of California, Colorado, Texas, Utah, and Nevada. The royal governors in Santa Fe did not care for outside influences to disturb the fragile peace they had managed to keep over the years between the American Indians and the local Spanish population.

The French were not the only ones who cast envious eyes toward New Mexico and the riches it held. In 1804, the very year that Meriwether Lewis and William Clark started their momentous journey to the Pacific Ocean, an American merchant—William Morrison of Kaskaskia, then in Indiana Territory—sent Jeannot Metoyer and Jean Baptiste LaLande up the Missouri River with orders to cut cross-country to New Mexico. They were followed the same year by Lorenzo Durocher and Jacques d'Eglise. All four men made it safely to Santa Fe and traded successfully with the

New Mexicans. LaLande even decided to stay in the remote village, and the hapless Morrison was left without his profits from the mission.

In 1805 James Purcell, a fur trapper from Kentucky, arrived in Santa Fe after spending close to three years in the trans-Mississippi wilderness. He liked the town and people so well that he permanently settled there and became a carpenter. He was still a resident when the next American to frequent the region, Lieutenant Zebulon Pike, arrived in early 1807. Pike had been placed in command of an expedition to explore the southwestern part of Louisiana Territory. During 1806–1807, Pike and his companions covered many miles of the region, and, among their other

Zebulon Pike. CHARLES WILLSON PEALE / PUBLIC DOMAIN

discoveries, they were the first Americans to view the famous mountain located in present-day Colorado, and later named Pike's Peak.

Pike's involvement with New Mexico began on July 15, 1806, when he and twenty-three soldiers under the orders of Louisiana Territory's governor, General James Wilkinson, left St. Louis, ostensibly to explore the headwaters of the Red River. In reality, General Wilkinson and his close associate, former vice president of the United States, Aaron Burr, privately nurtured dreams of creating a renegade Spanish-American government in which they would be the kingpins.

It was with this scheme in mind that Wilkinson dispatched Pike to the Far West with instructions to spy out the Spanish territories and towns of northern New Spain. In late February 1807, the Americans crossed the boundary that separated Louisiana from New Spain and were confronted by Spanish soldiers near the headwaters of the Rio Grande. When approached by the soldiers, Pike exclaimed, "What, is not this the Red River?" knowing full well that it was not. Although they were not officially arrested, Pike and his companions were marched to Santa Fe for an interview with the governor. History has failed to record just exactly how Lieutenant Pike expected to be received by authorities in Santa Fe as he rode into the village that long-ago day in early March 1807. The American army officer was accompanied by a company of colorfully uniformed Spanish dragoons, each decked out in a "short blue coat, with red cape and cuffs . . . and . . . a broad brimmed, high crowned wool hat,"[2] and armed with a carbine, pistol, and cutlass.

But history has preserved Pike's initial impression of Santa Fe. In the lengthy book which recorded his journey to New Mexico, entitled *An Account of Expeditions to the Sources of the Mississippi, and through the Western Parts of Louisiana*, Pike described the capital of Spain's northernmost province in North America as follows:

> *Its appearance, from a distance, struck my mind with the same effect as a fleet of the flat bottomed boats, which are seen in the spring and fall seasons, descending the Ohio River. There are two churches, the magnificence of whose steeples form a striking contrast to the miserable appearance of the houses. On the north side of the town is the square*

of soldiers' houses, equal to 120 or 140 on each flank. The public square is in the centre of the town; on the north side of which is situated the palace (as the[y] term it) or government house, with the quarters for guards, &c.[3]

Nearing the palace, Pike was confronted by a crowd of curious onlookers. He was obviously one of the few Americans that most of them had ever seen. Although his uniform, consisting of "blue trowsers, mockinsons, blanket coat and a cap made of scarlet cloth, lined with fox skins,"[4] was badly damaged and in disarray from his months of travel, the young lieutenant still cut a dashing figure. Dismounting at the palace, Pike was escorted into an anteroom where he awaited the governor's arrival.

Governor Joaquin del Real Alencaster minced no words. "Do you speak French?" he asked Pike. The lieutenant replied that he did, so the ensuing conversation was carried out in that language. The interview did not go well for Pike, and it appeared obvious to him that the governor was attempting to trap him into admitting that the real goal of his mission was to spy on the inhabitants and facilities of New Spain's northern frontier. In another interview later in the evening of the same day, Pike tried to assure Alencaster that he harbored "no hostile intentions toward the Spanish government." After reading Pike's army commission and orders, the governor "gave me his hand, for the first time, and said he was happy to be acquainted with me as a man of honor."[5]

On the following day, after examining the contents of Pike's trunk and finding incriminating letters, Governor Alencaster informed the American that he must be sent to Chihuahua to be interviewed by authorities there. "If we go to Chihuahua we must be considered as prisoners of war," asserted an exasperated Pike. "By no means," replied the official. "You will dine with me today, and march afterwards to a village about six miles distant . . . where the remainder of your escort is now waiting for you." From that point, Pike was informed that he would begin the long trip to Chihuahua. Before leaving the interview, the lieutenant was given a shirt and scarf made by the governor's sister, "and never worn by any person."[6] After dinner at the Palace of the Governors, which consisted of "a variety of dishes and wines of the southern provinces,"[7] the governor accompanied Pike to the outskirts of town, and the American headed south with the Spanish military escort.

Lieutenant Pike and his men made the journey to distant Chihuahua, and after friendly interrogation there, they were released later in the spring. When he returned to the United States, he reported from memory to an anxious General Wilkinson all that he had seen and heard in New Spain, and published the book that revealed his impressions of the wonders of the exotic territory he had visited.

Although Pike's glowing reports of what he had seen in the vastness of New Spain served only to whet the appetites of others who immediately planned trips to Santa Fe, the American lieutenant also recognized a downside to the region. His comments regarding the potential utility of the land through which he had passed were directly responsible for the creation and propagation of the "Great American Desert" myth that discouraged American immigration across the southern Great Plains for years. Reinforcing his opinion, he wrote in his book that the vast, treeless prairie would restrict "our population to some certain limits," and that

> *our citizens being so prone to rambling and extending themselves on the frontiers will, through necessity, be constrained to limit their extent on the west to the borders of the Missouri and Mississippi, while they leave the prairies incapable of cultivation to the wandering and uncivilized aborigines of the country.*[8]

Manuel Lisa, a well-known Missouri fur trapper and organizer of the Missouri Fur Company, became interested in Santa Fe in 1806. Lisa lent money to Jacques Clamorgan, a seventy-four-year-old fur entrepreneur from St. Louis, who, along with four companions and four mules loaded with trade goods, entered the Spanish town in December 1807, thus establishing himself as the first documented American trader to actually make money in the Santa Fe trade. After this initial attempt to break into a trading relationship with New Mexico, Lisa pursued interests elsewhere, but as late as 1812, he still nourished ambitions of establishing a large-scale business with Santa Fe. In a letter dated September 8, 1812, addressed to the "Spaniards of New Mexico," Lisa wrote, "Ever since my first journey among the forks of the Missouri, nine-hundred leagues from my domicile, I have desired to find an opportunity to communicate with my [com]patriots, the Spaniards." Continuing, Lisa told his correspondents that he was sending the present letter via a trusted lieutenant, Don Carlos Sanguinet, and that he had instructed Sanguinet:

> to arrange that this letter . . . should fall into the hands of some Spaniard who may be worthy to communicate with me on those honorable principles, and in no other manner, my desire being to engage in business and open up a new commerce, which might easily be done. With this in view, and as a director of the Missouri Fur Company, I propose to you gentlemen that if you wish to trade and deal with me, for whatever quantity of goods it may be, I will obligate myself to fill each year any bill of goods which shall be given me, and all shall be delivered (as stipulated) both as to quality and as to quantity, at the place nearest and most convenient for both parties, to your satisfaction, after we shall have agreed on the chosen place.[9]

Manuel Lisa's destiny lay on the headwaters of the Missouri River, however, and it was up to other men to pursue the opening of the Santa Fe trade in earnest.

Over the next ten years or so, several other parties of Missouri traders made trips to Santa Fe. However, because Spanish authorities there were hostile toward Americans and wary of their intense interest in the region, most of the traders were arrested and their goods confiscated.

One of the most bizarre incidents to occur during the early American attempts to open the door to the Santa Fe trade involved three Missouri traders named Robert McKnight, Samuel Chambers, and James Baird. The men left St. Louis in the spring of 1812, and when they arrived in Santa Fe later that year, they were promptly arrested by the Spanish, and their trading goods were seized. Not only were most members of the expedition imprisoned until 1821, when the Mexicans won their independence from Spain, but the poor souls were invoiced for their

A Trapper (An Old Time Trapper). FREDERIC REMINGTON / PUBLIC DOMAIN

own upkeep while in jail, at the cost of 18¾ cents per day, to be charged against the trade goods they had brought with them.

In September 1815, two other St. Louis fur men, Auguste P. Chouteau and Jules de Mun, left St. Louis for the headwaters of the Arkansas River, where they intended to trade with the Arapaho Indians. Due to the lateness of the season, among other things, the venture was less than successful. De Mun returned to St. Louis, outfitted a new party, and went back to the mountains on July 15, 1816. During May of the following year, the trapping outfit was confronted by Spanish soldiers who arrested the entire lot and carried them to Santa Fe, where they were imprisoned. De Mun explained his plight in a letter written in November 1817 to William Clark, the governor of Missouri Territory:

> *Having to relate to your excellency the unfortunate event which has thrown me, Mr. Auguste P. Chouteau, and twenty-four men, forty-eight days, in the dungeons of Santa Fe, and which, by depriving us of every thing we possessed, has brought us to the brink of ruin, I must beg your excellency's indulgence if I take too much of your time. But I think myself bound to give a detailed account of what has happened; the more so, as your excellency's right of granting us a license to go to the headwaters of the Arkansas and Platte rivers was denied by the Governor of New Mexico.*[10]

After De Mun offered a lengthy and detailed description of the events leading up to and including the arrest and imprisonment, during which time the men were held in irons for forty-five days, he concluded his letter to Clark:

> *[T]he Governor acknowledged to me afterwards . . . that we were very innocent men; yet, notwithstanding this, all our property was kept, and we were permitted to come home, each with one of the worst horses we had. . . . Our actual loss amounts to $30,380.74½. The benefits which we had a probable, indeed a most assured, confidence to reap from our labors, would no doubt have fully compensated us. It remains now to know whether our Government will demand satisfaction of the King of Spain for outrages committed by his ignorant Governor on American citizens.*[11]

Three other Americans journeyed to New Mexico during 1820. Nineteen-year-old David Meriwether was accompanied by a few Pawnee Indians, led by their chief, Big Elk, and a black cook named Alfred. Meriwether, born in Virginia and raised in Kentucky, was a distant kinsman of

Meriwether Lewis of Lewis and Clark fame. Meriwether was experienced for his age; the previous year he had hired out to Colonel John O'Fallon of St. Louis as a trader and sutler for Colonel Henry Atkinson's 1819–1820 Yellowstone Expedition. Following his service with Atkinson on the upper Missouri, at which time he met his companion, Alfred, Meriwether returned to Council Bluffs, anxious to make a trip to New Mexico to investigate stories of abundant gold there, told to the Pawnees by a captured Mexican and his son.

While pausing for the evening on a tributary of the Canadian River, Meriwether was looking about for a campsite when he noticed many horse and mule tracks in the sand and mud. Alarmed, he reported the animal tracks to his Indian companions and suggested that they probably should move on and camp elsewhere. When Big Elk returned from studying the stream bank himself, however, he declared that the tracks were old and that their presence posed no danger. Unconvinced, Meriwether and Alfred crossed the stream and pitched their camp among the hills several hundred yards away.

The following morning at dawn, the sound of gunfire awakened Meriwether and Alfred. The Pawnees who had accompanied the party—and who, despite Meriwether's apprehensions, had spent the night on the riverbank—were under attack. Shortly afterward, when Big Elk and another brave rode into Meriwether's camp, he told the alarmed American that Spanish soldiers had raided his camp, killing most of the other Pawnees.

Under a flag of truce, Meriwether and Alfred ventured toward the Spanish encampment, where they were immediately disarmed and stripped of all valuables. On the following day, the two men were marched westward, on foot, by the soldiers. When told to move on after a rest stop, Meriwether refused to walk any further, due to his sore feet. At last, he was given a mule to ride.

Several days later, the entourage arrived in Santa Fe, where Meriwether was presented to the governor. After a brief audience, since the American could speak no Spanish and the governor could speak no English, Meriwether was thrown into a prison cell, "with only a small window about the size of a pane of eight by ten glass to admit a little fresh air and light."[12]

Following a couple of days of prison life, during which time he "thought the bed bugs and fleas would eat me up,"[13] Meriwether was visited by a French-speaking priest. Since the young American also spoke French, he could now complete that interview with the governor. With the priest acting as interpreter, Meriwether attempted to explain the purpose of his visit to the disbelieving official. Thrown back into jail, Meriwether spent several more days in the squalor of his dark cell before his friend, the priest, again visited him. Then, in another interview with the governor, Meriwether was more or less placed under house arrest, whereby he was free to explore the town in the daytime, but obliged to report back to jail at night. Later still, the governor allowed Meriwether to be free altogether, as long as the priest could account for his whereabouts.

As autumn approached, Meriwether was hired by an old Mexican man to help harvest peppers and beans from his garden. Then, "one evening this good priest came in and said he had good news for me; he had had a long conversion with the Governor that day, and he thought that I would be permitted to return to my friends very shortly."[14] On the following day, in yet another interview with the governor, Meriwether was told he could return to the United States if he promised never to enter New Mexico again.

Vowing to follow the governor's orders, Meriwether and Alfred, with enough supplies to get them back to the United States, left Santa Fe. After spending an extremely cold winter on the Great Plains, during which time the two men nearly starved and froze to death, the pair reached the Pawnee villages in February 1821. The following month, they arrived at their final destination, Council Bluffs.

Eventually, David Meriwether returned to the area around Louisville, Kentucky, where he married and sired thirteen children. He pursued various business interests until 1852, when, in June, he was appointed to fill the vacant seat in the US Senate left by the death of Henry Clay. In 1853 he consented to break his thirty-year-old promise never to return to New Mexico, when he was summoned to the White House and prevailed upon by President Franklin Pierce to become the governor of that faraway land.

During the years since Meriwether first traveled there in 1820, the country had won its independence from Spain, only to be occupied by the American army in the late war with Mexico. Now an American territory, it was in need of a governor who understood the land and its people, and who could peacefully settle the boundary-line dispute between the two nations. Meriwether served his adopted territory well at an extremely difficult time in its existence. Animosities between the United States and Mexico remained, the border dispute was still up in the air, and Indians continued to create problems for the new American government. But Meriwether endured the storm, serving as governor until 1857, when he resigned and returned to Kentucky.

The trials and tribulations of the third American to make the long trip to New Mexico during 1820 are not so well documented as those of Meriwether and Alfred. He was Joseph R. Walker, a Tennessean who had migrated to Missouri and later rose to prominence as the first American to view Yosemite, and the leader of the first wagon train to California. About all that is known is that Walker was arrested in Santa Fe and detained there before being returned to his Missouri home. He later became involved in the survey of the Santa Fe Trail, and his contributions will be picked up in a later chapter.

The routes taken to Santa Fe by most of these earlier explorers and traders did not always follow the path of the later Santa Fe Trail in its totality. However, at least portions of the Trail were either crossed or traveled to some degree by some or all of these people. Pedro Vial, for example, used portions of the Trail in his several travels across the southern Great Plains, and others, no doubt, did so as well.

Over the years, regardless of how hard they tried, American traders had little luck bringing free trade to the remote towns of New Mexico. Finally, in 1821, an event in Mexico City provided the incentive needed for New Mexicans to dismantle the trade barriers that had intimidated Americans and kept them away for so long. And, that same event induced certain American traders back in Missouri to blaze the thoroughfare that would soon become known as the Santa Fe Trail across the southern Great Plains.

CHAPTER THREE

Trails West!

WHEN CHRISTOPHER COLUMBUS ACCIDENTALLY STUMBLED UPON THE New World in 1492, thinking that he had really discovered a new way to reach the Far East, he set the stage for years to come for Spanish domination over most of the Western Hemisphere.

By 1493 the Pope in Rome had divided up the so-called New World between Portugal and Spain—at the time, the two most successful seafaring nations in the world. All of the land west of an imaginary line, which was drawn from the North Pole to the South Pole through the Atlantic Ocean, henceforth belonged to Spain. Included in this vast domain of uncharted land and water were both continents of North and South America, except for present-day Brazil, which was given to Portugal.

Most of the land originally claimed by Spain remained in its possession for many years. Eventually, however, other European powers staked out parts of the New World. Various groups of English settled up and down the Eastern Seaboard of North America, from New England to Georgia. The French explored and claimed for their own the northern expanses of the continent, including most of today's country of Canada, as well as large portions of what would later become the United States. And, seafarers from the Netherlands colonized a small area around New York City.

But the vast majority of both North and South America remained under the control of Spain. Other Spanish explorers quickly followed Columbus. Hernán Cortés landed on the Mexican shore in 1519, and his countryman Francisco Pizarro explored Peru in 1532. Hernando de Soto traveled extensively throughout the southeastern United States beginning in 1539, while Francisco Vázquez de Coronado did likewise in the Southwest in 1540. The presence of these men among—and, in the case of Cortés and Pizarro, their destruction of—the numerous American Indian tribes they encountered solidified for all time the Spanish yoke of conquest in a large segment of the New World.

Such were the conditions, then, in Mexico during the early years of the nineteenth century, when a few Americans—primarily Missourians—began eyeing Santa Fe and other New Mexican towns as possible outlets for their trade goods.

So far, Americans had not had a great deal of luck in breaking down the trade barriers with Mexico, primarily due to the suspicions that Spanish authorities had for anyone from the outside world who expressed an interest in Mexico and the rest of New Spain. And, of course, everyone in Missouri was familiar with the lurid stories of their friends who had tried to unlock the door to Mexican trade in years gone by and, as a result of their persistence, were rewarded with years of unfair imprisonment.

In 1821, however, an incident occurred in New Spain that dramatically changed the attitudes that government officials and the common people of Mexico had for Americans. After years of unsuccessful attempts, Mexico finally won its independence from Spain and flung open its doors to any and all Americans who wished to trade with her people. Missourians, of course, were delighted over the news. By the fall, one of them, William Becknell, a native Virginian in his early thirties, entered the fabled town of Santa Fe to try his hand at trading in what everyone back home thought to be a fabulously rich country.

Becknell had migrated to Missouri in 1810 and settled on land just west of the village of St. Charles. The following year he was operating a ferry at Arrow Rock. During the War of 1812, he served as a mounted ranger in Daniel Morgan Boone's company and after limited action was discharged in 1815. He then bought two town lots in Franklin, operated a saltworks for a while, and eventually borrowed money to buy a farm in Howard County. In 1820, when elections were conducted for state officials to guide Missouri's entrance into the Union, Becknell was unsuccessful in his quest for a seat in the House of Representatives. By the following year, he had resolved to become a trader, his decision no doubt partially based on persistent rumors that were currently circulating about Mexico's newest move for independence.

Becknell correctly assessed the sketchy news from Santa Fe that an overthrow of the Spanish government was imminent. Accordingly, he organized a trading company whose purpose was to trade "Horses & Mules and catching Wild Animals of every description, that we think advantageous to the company." In late June 1821, some three months before news of Mexico's independence had reached Missouri, Becknell advertised in the Franklin *Missouri Intelligencer* for men to accompany him on his company's first commercial endeavor, a journey to the Far West, perhaps even to the frontiers of New Mexico. The advertisement read, in part:

> *Every man will fit himself for the trip with a horse, a good rifle, and as much ammunition as the company may think necessary for a tour or 3 month trip, & sufficient cloathing [sic] to keep him warm and comfortable. Every man will furnish his equal part of the fitting on for our trade, and receive an equal part of the product. If the company consist of 30 or more men, 10 dollars a man will answer to purchase the quantity of merchandise required to trade on.*
>
> *No man shall receive more than another for his services, unless he furnishes more, and is pointedly agreed on by the company before we start. . . . There will be no dividend until we return to the north side of the Missouri river, where all persons concerned shall have timely notice to attend and receive their share of the profits. . . . It is requisite that every 8 men shall have a pack horse, an ax, and a tent to secure them from the inclemency of bad weather. . . . It shall be my business to apply to the governor for permission to proceed as far as we wish to go. Signers to the amount of 70 will be received until the 4th of August, when every man wishing to go is requested to meet at Ezekiel Williams's on the Missouri, about five miles above Franklin, where we will procure a pilot and appoint officers to the company.*[1]

Although Becknell's advertisement suggests that he was hoping for a sizable response, his party, when he set out from Arrow Rock, Missouri, on September 1, 1821, apparently consisted of only three or four men and as many mules, each animal laden with trade goods. Only recently, and still unbeknownst to anyone in the United States, Mexico had declared its independence from Spain. Becknell's departure marks the real beginnings of American commercialism with New Mexico, and because of his premier role in the historic event, he is sometimes called by modern scholars the "father" of the Santa Fe trade.

Becknell's outward journey carried his small party along what is recognized as the primary, or mountain, route of the Santa Fe Trail. From the Missouri settlements, the traders entered present-day Kansas. Moving southwestward, they passed the future town sites of Council Grove, Fort Larned, and Dodge City. Following the Arkansas River, they

Confrontation between William Becknell and Mexican soldiers. COURTESY OF JAMES A. CRUTCHFIELD

crossed into present-day Colorado and cut a thoroughfare southwestward to Raton Pass on today's Colorado–New Mexico border.

By the time Becknell's party was about two weeks away from Santa Fe and located somewhere in northern New Mexico, they ran into snow. Becknell later wrote:

> *Having been now travelling about fifty days, our diet being altogether different from what we had been accustomed to; and unexpected hardships and obstacles occurring almost daily, our company is much discouraged; but the prospect of a near termination of our journey excites hope and redoubled exertion, although our horses are so reduced that we only travel from eight to fifteen miles per day. We found game scarce near the mountains, and one night encamped without wood or water.*[2]

As they neared their destination in November 1821, Becknell and his party were approached by soldiers. Apprehensive about what might occur, the Missourians watched carefully as the troops drew nearer. But, thankfully, the soldiers warmly greeted Becknell and his men and welcomed them to the newly independent country of Mexico. Becknell later poetically recalled that:

> *Although the difference of our language would not admit of conversation, yet the circumstances attending their reception of us, fully convinced us of their friendly feelings. Being likewise in a strange country, and subject to their disposition, our wishes lent their aid to increase our confidence in their manifestations of kindness.*[3]

Becknell soon confirmed that the Mexican people had recently won their independence from Spain. He was further told that the new government would not only tolerate free trade with Americans, but that it would actually seek it. What a relief this news must have been to Becknell and his men, as they traveled the short remainder of their journey to Santa Fe.

Becknell later met in the capital city with the governor, Don Facundo Melgares, and reveals in his journal that the official "expressed a desire that Americans would keep up an intercourse with that country, and said that if any of them wished to emigrate, it would give him pleasure to afford them every facility."[4]

After Becknell had depleted his limited supply of trading goods, he stayed around Santa Fe for a brief time, observing the residents, their mode of farming, and the countryside in general. While not overly impressed with the region or its inhabitants, he took the time to observe the agricultural attributes of New Mexico, and later wrote:

> Corn, rice and wheat are their principal production; they have very few garden vegetables except the onion, which grows large and abundantly; the seeds are planted nearly a foot apart, and produce onions from four to six inches in diameter. Their atmosphere is remarkably dry, and rain is uncommon except in the months of July and August. To remedy this inconvenience, they substitute, with tolerable advantage, the numerous streams which descend from the mountains, by daming [sic] them up, and conveying the water over their farms in ditches. Their domestic animals consist chiefly of sheep, goats, mules, and asses. None but the wealthy have horses and hogs.[5]

In early December Becknell finally left New Mexico and made the trip back to Franklin, Missouri, in a record forty-eight days. There must have been great celebration in Franklin when Becknell came riding into town on January 30, 1822, after his long and tiring trek to Santa Fe and back. Years later a neighbor reported:

> My father saw them unload when they returned, and when their rawhide packages of silver dollars were dumped on the sidewalk one of the men cut the thongs and the money spilled out and clinking on the stone pavement rolled into the gutter. Everyone was excited and the next spring another expedition was sent out.[6]

The new "expedition" that was to leave Missouri the following May was planned to be a much more grandiose affair than Becknell's original trading party. This time wagons, instead of mules, would be used to carry the freight, and this decision brought with it logistical problems not encountered on the first trip. But, hardships aside, Becknell had already decided to be a part of this larger, second mission.

William Becknell wasted no time after he returned to Missouri in getting his second expedition in order. At this point, it was already apparent that he had no monopoly on the Santa Fe trade. In fact, the previous season, when he had made his first trip, two other parties had entered Santa Fe immediately after he had. One was led by trappers named Hugh Glenn and Jacob Fowler. The other, a trading expedition, included Thomas James and John McKnight, the brother of Robert McKnight, who had tried his hand at dealing with officials of New Spain years earlier only to be imprisoned in Mexico for his efforts.

Neither of the competitor groups had traveled along the Santa Fe Trail in order to arrive at their destination. The Thomas James–John McKnight party had ascended the Arkansas River by boat from the Mississippi River to the Cimarron. Then, on horseback they followed that river for about two hundred miles before reaching the North Fork of the Canadian River. Proceeding from there in a southerly direction, the party struck the Canadian River a few miles north of present-day Amarillo, Texas. Following the Canadian westward brought the traders to today's New Mexico–Texas border, whence they journeyed westward again to San Miguel and, finally, Santa Fe.

In the meantime, the Jacob Fowler–Hugh Glenn party had left Fort Smith and followed the Arkansas River to trap the region around today's Pueblo, Colorado. From there, after learning from some Spanish soldiers that Mexico had gained its independence and now welcomed American trappers and traders, Glenn took a few men with him and journeyed to Santa Fe from the north.

For three and a half months after his first return from Santa Fe, Becknell and his associates prepared for their more-complex, larger, second expedition. Finally, when all was ready, Becknell left Franklin and, on May 22, 1822, crossed the Missouri River on the Arrow Rock ferry. Three days later he departed Fort Osage with twenty-one men and three wagons full of top-quality trade goods, bound for Santa Fe.

Becknell felt as much competitive pressure on this trip as he had on the journey the previous year. Colonel Benjamin Cooper, with fifteen men, had just proceeded from the Missouri settlements several days earlier, before Becknell and his group could get under way. Although surely Becknell and other traders about to enter the Santa Fe trade realized that there was enough business for everyone, each wanted to be absolutely sure he got to the fabled town on the far end of the Trail first in order to obtain the choicest New Mexican products—mules, silver, and furs—that the natives had to offer.

About one month after he had left Fort Osage, Becknell and his followers ran into the first of several troublesome incidents that occurred during the second journey. He later wrote of the event:

> *About midnight our horses were frightened by buffaloes, and all strayed—28 were missing. Eight of us, after appointing a place of rendezvous, went in pursuit of them in different directions, and found eighteen.*[7]

While hunting for the horses, two of the men were captured by Osage Indians and roughed up a bit, but were later released. All of the pair's equipment, which had been stolen by the Indians, was returned, and Becknell elected not to retaliate upon the band of Osage that had caused the havoc.

Because he had wagons with him this time, Becknell knew that his party could not negotiate the steep cliffs and rock outcroppings that were common throughout Raton Pass on the Colorado–New Mexico border. There was simply no easy way for the cumbersome and heavily loaded wagons to proceed through such rough and treacherous country. Accordingly, when he arrived in the neighborhood of today's Dodge City, Kansas, Becknell diverted from the route that he had taken the previous year and set a course toward the southwest and across the dry region that lay between the Arkansas and Cimarron Rivers.

The new route, which in later years was called the Cimarron Cutoff, crossed some extremely desolate and dry country. Josiah Gregg, the merchant and writer who traveled extensively on the Santa Fe Trail some

Fort Osage. GEORGE FULLER GREEN / PUBLIC DOMAIN

years later, wrote of a harrowing incident that occurred on the Cutoff in his 1844 book, *Commerce of the Prairies*:

> *The adventurous band pursued their forward course without being able to procure any water, except from the scanty supply they carried in their canteens. As this source of relief was completely exhausted after two days' march, the sufferings of both men and beasts had driven them almost to distraction. The forlorn band were at last reduced to the cruel necessity of killing their dogs, and cutting off the ears of their mules, in the vain hope of assuaging their burning thirst with hot blood. This only served to irritate the parched palates, and madden the senses of the sufferers. Frantic with despair, in prospect of the horrible death which now stared them in the face, they scattered in every direction in search of that element which they had left behind them in such abundance, but without success.*[8]

After several grueling days of blistering heat and unquenchable thirst, Becknell's expedition finally made it to the far side of the desert. A few more days' travel, after satisfying their need for water, found them first in the New Mexican village of San Miguel, not far from Santa Fe, then shortly afterward, in the capital city itself.

Interested in lightening his load on the return trip to Missouri, Becknell not only disposed of all of his trading goods, but sold one of his wagons as well. The vehicle had cost him $150 back home, but records indicate that he sold it in Santa Fe for $700. It is estimated that Becknell realized a 2,000 percent profit on the wares that he sold to the New Mexicans during this second trading venture to Santa Fe.

Becknell was not happy about the strenuous ordeal that he and his men had endured on the journey out from Missouri. Thoughts of the thirst and extreme heat haunted him constantly. Accordingly, when he returned, he took a different route, the exact path of which is unknown today. Becknell, thus, "considerably shortened the route, and arrived at Fort Osage in 48 days."[9] No doubt the return trip was made somewhere in the vicinity of the outbound journey, since the trail through the Cimarron Cutoff was by then known to be considerably shorter than any other course.

The next time William Becknell visited New Mexico was in late 1824, but on this occasion he came as a fur trapper instead of a trader. Eastern goods had flooded into Santa Fe during the past three years, and apparently Becknell thought that a fur-trapping trip into the Colorado and Wyoming Rockies would pay better returns than another trading mission to New Mexico.

In any event, Becknell left Missouri for the third time in August 1824, and by November was in Santa Cruz, a small village north of Santa Fe. From there, he left for the planned trip north, but winter caught him and his party before they could make much headway. The cold was intense, and Becknell later remembered:

> We suffered every misery incident to such an enterprise in the winter season, such as hunger and cold. . . . The flesh of a very lean horse, which we were constrained to break our fast with, was at this time, pronounced excellent.[10]

Becknell and his party left the horrors of the Rocky Mountain winter in early 1825, and by April they had arrived back in New Mexico, whence they proceeded home to Missouri. Now disgruntled with the harsh realities of fur trapping, Becknell dropped his second career as rapidly as he had his first.

But Becknell stayed involved with the infant Santa Fe Trail for at least a little while longer. By the time he had returned from his third trip to New Mexico, many residents of Missouri had petitioned the US Congress to mark the road to Santa Fe and to make improvements upon it that would enhance its use as a trade route. When funds were allocated for the project in 1825, the commissioners who were appointed to oversee the survey turned to Becknell, not only for his advice on the actual routing of the Trail, but to furnish fresh stock and supplies to the survey parties as well.

CHAPTER FOUR

Surveying the Trail

THE MAN MOST DIRECTLY RESPONSIBLE FOR THE UNITED STATES GOV-
ernment survey of the Santa Fe Trail was Senator Thomas Hart Benton
of Missouri. During the 1824–1825 session of Congress, Benton argued
that a clearly defined and protected Santa Fe Trail would benefit all
parties concerned—the Mexicans at the far end, the Indians through
whose territory the Trail passed, and, certainly, the Americans who were
exploiting the Santa Fe trade with increasing frequency.

Several years later, when Benton compiled his memoirs, he explained
the logic in pursuing the survey of the Santa Fe Trail, writing in 1854 that:

*The name of Mexico, the synonym of gold and silver mines, possessed
always an invincible charm for the people of the western states. . . .
It was not until the Independence of Mexico, in the year 1821, that
the frontiers of this vast and hitherto sealed up country were thrown
open to foreign ingress, and trade and intercourse allowed to take their
course. The State of Missouri, from her geographical position, and the
adventurous spirit of her inhabitants, was among the first to engage
in it. . . . In three years it had grown to be a new and regular branch
of interior commerce, profitable to those engaged in it, valuable to the
country from the articles it carried out, and for the silver, the furs,
and the mules which it brought back; and well entitled to the protection and care of the government. That protection was sought . . . in
the form . . . of . . . a right of way through the countries of the tribes
between Missouri and New Mexico, a road marked out and security*

in travelling it, stipulations for good behavior from the Indians, and a consular establishment in the provinces to be traded with.[1]

Benton's bill for the survey of the Santa Fe Trail passed the Senate by a vote of thirty to twelve, and it sailed through the House of Representatives with thirty votes to spare. On March 3, 1825, James Monroe, in one of his last acts as president of the United States, signed the legislation authorizing the survey into law. A sum of $10,000 was appropriated for the expense of the survey itself. An additional $20,000 was set aside for the purchase of gifts for the Indians who resided in the region in exchange for the road's right-of-way through their territory.

Shortly after President Monroe signed the survey bill, the new president, John Quincy Adams, appointed three men to serve as commissioners for the project. All three were eminently qualified for the job. Benjamin H. Reeves was the lieutenant governor of Missouri and a resident of Howard County, the hub of the Santa Fe Trail traffic on the eastern end. Pierre Menard, a resident of Kaskaskia, Illinois, and a longtime fur trader and partner in the Missouri Fur Company, turned down the opportunity to be a commissioner due to other pressing business matters. He was promptly replaced by Thomas Mather, an Illinois legislator and descendant of the famed New England churchman, Cotton Mather. Finally, George C. Sibley, the government factor at Fort Osage since the post opened for business in 1808, was tapped as the third member of what was now being called the Santa Fe Road Commission.

The next matter at hand was the selection by the commission members of a competent surveyor, a secretary, and crew members to assist in the mission. Joseph C. Brown, a surveyor by profession and a member of the Missouri senate, was chosen as the actual surveyor. Archibald Gamble, a St. Louis banker and circuit court clerk, was picked for the secretary's position. Later commenting on these two appointments, Commissioner Sibley wrote:

Mr. Brown was preferred to all his competitors without a moment's hesitation, as being in the opinion of the Commrs [Commissioners]

Thomas Hart Benton. FROM *THIRTY YEARS IN THE US SENATE* / PUBLIC DOMAIN

best qualified in all respects. Mr. Gamble's pretensions for Secy [Secretary] were thought at least equal to those of any other applicant; and he was preferred because he was accustomed to the business of surveying with Mr. Brown.[2]

Stephen Cooper, a Santa Fe trade veteran, was picked to be the pilot, and Joseph R. Walker, whose name in years to come would be indelibly linked with the early exploration of California, was hired as a hunter and chainman (those who measured distances for the surveyor). William

Sherley "Old Bill" Williams, a noted Rocky Mountain fur trapper, was appointed interpreter. Joseph Walker's brother, Joel, who is generally credited with later taking the first American settlers to California, also was hired, along with Kit Carson's half-brother, Andrew, and several others. All in all, the list of those who worked on the Santa Fe Road Commission at one time or another reads like a "Who's Who" of Western exploration.

The commissioners chose Fort Osage on the Missouri River, near present-day Kansas City, Missouri, as the beginning point for their work. No one knew exactly what lay ahead of the survey party or what difficulties would be encountered before the men reached Santa Fe. Of the challenges, the *Missouri Republican* reported that:

> *The hot weather, the number of flies and the difficulty of getting their wagons through a tractless [sic] country will oblige them to travel slow, and it will be sometime [sic] before they complete the work. The Commissioners say twelve or thirteen months.*[3]

By July 17, 1825, all was ready at Fort Osage, and the caravan headed west. The survey team now consisted of seven baggage wagons, fifty-seven horses and mules, and forty men. All members were well aware of the importance of the survey. Just two weeks earlier, Senator Benton had reminded Sibley of the significance that the results had to the country. "The main idea," he wrote, "is thoroughness, for it is not a County or State road which they have to mark out but a highway between Nations."[4]

When the survey party had traveled about three weeks out of Fort Osage, it reached the Neosho River, the site of present-day Council Grove, Kansas. There, the commissioners met with the Osage Indians. For $300 worth of merchandise and $500 credit, the Osage promised safe passage for future American traffic through the tribe's territory. On August 16 a similar treaty was signed with representatives of the Kansas tribe.

By September 11 the surveyors had arrived at the upper reaches of the Arkansas River, which then served as the boundary line between Mexico and the United States. In the absence of specific instructions on how to proceed across Mexican territory, the party pitched camp on the American side of the river and awaited further orders. When, nine days later, no orders had arrived, Sibley suggested that two of the commissioners return to Missouri and that the other one proceed to Santa Fe. According to Sibley's journal, the matter was voted upon and:

> *I was designated by my Colleagues to go to Santa Fee [sic], and to make Selection of nine men, two Waggons & 19 Horses, and such Goods & Stores as I thought proper. It was then decided that Cols. Reeves & Mather Should tomorrow set out on their return to Missouri, with the rest of the Party. . . . Cols. Reeves & Mather are to join me at Santa Fee, as early as they can next summer (if the whole road is to be completed) that I am to wait for them 'till the 1st of July, and then if I hear nothing from them or the Govt [Government] to justify any longer delay, I am to return to Missouri as soon as I can.*[5]

On the following day, September 21, 1825, Commissioners Reeves and Mather and their respective parties started back for Missouri. Sibley remained in camp for the rest of the evening and began his trip to Santa Fe on the next day. With his group were the surveyor Joseph Brown and "Old Bill" Williams, among others. With surprisingly little difficulty, Sibley and his party trekked through the badlands of the Cimarron Cutoff, and when they reached the far side, he decided to proceed to Taos instead of trying to reach Santa Fe via San Miguel.

From Taos, Sibley moved on to Santa Fe, where he spent the winter of 1825–1826. During his sojourn in the capital, he became close friends with the New Mexican governor, Antonio Narbona. Late spring 1826 arrived before Mexican authorities finally gave their approval for Sibley to continue his survey of the Mexican end of the Santa Fe Trail. Sibley, now back in Taos, awaited the arrival of the other two commissioners. By the last week of August, when it was apparent that Reeves and Mather were not coming, Sibley and his remaining party started for home, marking the roadway as they went. By early October, Sibley had returned to Missouri, where he planned to meet with the other two commissioners and file their report with the government.

George Sibley. COURTESY OF JAMES A. CRUTCHFIELD

At about the same time that the survey was being accomplished by the Americans, a move was made by Mexican authorities that underscored their interest in seeing a successful trade route established between the United States and Santa Fe. The governor of New Mexico sent a special envoy up the Trail to its eastern terminus at Franklin, Missouri, and beyond, to St. Louis. The envoy, Manuel Simon Escudero, met with the United States Indian agent at St. Louis and made him aware that the purpose of his visit was to obtain protection from the Plains Indians in American territory who might harass Mexican traders utilizing the

Santa Fe Trail. Escudero was sent to Washington, DC, with his message but was rebuffed there by the Mexican minister for bypassing official political protocol.

Although nothing came of this effort on Mexico's part to negotiate with the United States, the incident does point out that by this early date, Mexican authorities were already thinking about utilizing the Trail as a west-to-east highway for their own traders, just as Americans were using it for an east-to-west thoroughfare for themselves.

On January 20, 1827, the three commissioners gathered in St. Louis, at which time Reeves and Mather turned over all responsibility for completing the report to Sibley. A second trip along the Santa Fe Trail was planned in order to make corrections. Colonel Reeves could not make the journey on account of his wife's illness, and Colonel Mather declined to go. The resurvey effort got under way in mid-May and consisted of twelve men, fourteen mules, one horse, and one wagon. When the party reached Diamond Spring, near the headwaters of the Neosho River, Sibley signaled the men to begin their return eastward. Near the end of October, the three commissioners met in St. Charles, Missouri, and approved the final repot of the survey. The document was signed by all three men and was then dispatched to authorities in Washington.

As it turned out, the Santa Fe Trail survey did little practical good. The final report revealed a minimum of new information that active Missouri traders did not already know. But, the news sounded good to the politicians in far-off Washington, and no doubt they believed they had received their money's worth when they read the commissioners' glowing report:

> *The Road, in nearly its whole extent, passes over open, grassy prairie; the forest or timber land, over which it Runs does not exceed altogether twenty Miles—Water, fuel, and pasturage are Sufficiently plentiful, and, with but few exceptions are good. Caravans may obtain their chief Supplies of Subsistence, without difficulty or delay, from the numerous herds of Buffaloes that are almost continually passing and repassing over the plains, crossing the Route everywhere along the*

greater part of the way; and many years must elapse before this great Resource will fail, or materially diminish.

Between Ft. Osage & San Fernando [Taos], there does not exist a Single Serious difficulty or obstacle to the passage of carriages of any description. Even the Mountains near Taus [sic] (where Scarcely any effort has ever yet been made to form a Road) are crossed without any great difficulty; and whenever the authorities there Shall think fit to order it, an excellent Road may be made at a very trifling expense. . . .

In Short, it may Safely be assumed that there are fewer natural obstructions between Ft. Osage and the City of Mexico, a distance not much Short of 2,500 Miles, than there are on the established Road from Ft. Osage to St. Louis, which is probably not inferior to any (except turnpikes) in the Union.[6]

For the next few years after the Santa Fe Trail survey was completed, traffic along the route moved briskly. During the decade between 1826 and 1835, more than 1,500 men accompanied 775 wagons carrying $1,365,000 worth of merchandise over the Trail. Americans had found a trader's paradise in New Mexico. Since the inhabitants of Santa Fe and the surrounding villages were isolated by great distances from the large towns of Mexico, they had to rely on their own skills and industry to make a meager living off the dry and sparse land. Trade caravans from Mexico City and other towns to the south were few and far between, but when American traders arrived on the scene with all kinds of hard-to-find goods, the common folk embraced them enthusiastically.

CHAPTER FIVE

Freighting on the Santa Fe Trail

IN 1821, AND EVEN MORE SO IN 1822, WILLIAM BECKNELL PROVED ONCE and for all that a lucrative business existed over the Santa Fe Trail between the Missouri settlements and the small towns and villages of New Mexico. His discovery set off a chain of events that eventually made the Trail the most frequented highway of commerce in the United States, with a popularity that spanned more than fifty years.

The advent of the Santa Fe Trail brought into being an entirely new occupation for adventurous men who wanted to cash in on the rich rewards to be reaped from trading with the New Mexicans. *Freighting* was what the new business was called, and before the heyday of the Trail was over, hundreds of individuals had become involved with the job of hauling freight of all descriptions from Missouri to Santa Fe.

William Becknell had used pack horses to haul his trade goods across the Trail on that very first trip back in 1821. But he soon realized that he could make more money if he could carry more merchandise on each trip, so from then on, Becknell and the rest of the Missourians used wagons, which held much more freight. At first, Conestoga wagons, large cloth-covered vehicles, were used. Later versions of these wagons could carry upward of six thousand pounds.

In the early days of Trail activity, mules were used to pull the big Conestogas, but after Major Bennet Riley successfully demonstrated the adaptability of oxen for the task, these animals grew in popularity. Oxen could pull almost as well as mules, and they were a great deal cheaper. Horses were rarely used to haul freight wagons, since they did not possess the stamina of mules and oxen, plus the fact that they were more sensitive to heat, thirst, and disease. They also cost more to feed.

Two mules formed a span, and in the 1840s a span of mules cost from around $200 to $400. A pair of oxen was called a yoke, and, during the same period, cost somewhere between $20 and $30. In addition to their economic advantage, oxen could be killed in emergency situations and eaten, just like beef. The only drawback with oxen was that they tended to be a little bit slower than mules. Oxen, on a good day, could travel about twelve to fifteen miles, while mules might make fifteen to twenty.

All kinds of merchandise was hauled by the freighters. The New Mexicans were anxious to get their hands on any type of Eastern goods, few of which could be obtained from sources in Mexico City. Needles, thread, buttons, and other sewing notions; nails, axes, shovels, and log chains; dry goods consisting of silk, flannel, and calico; manufactured goods such as pants, suspenders, dresses, and shirts; as well as beads, scissors, razors, and a thousand other items for home and farm found themselves in the traders' wagons.

In return for all of these wonderful goods, the New Mexicans gladly swapped gold and silver coins, gold dust, silver bullion, rich beaver furs, finely woven woolen blankets, mules, and donkeys. And the Missourians always seemed to get the better end of the bargain. In 1824 one American trader carried $30,000 worth of merchandise with him to Santa Fe and returned with Mexican goods that made him a clear profit of $150,000.

A typical trading mission had its beginning in one of the Missouri settlements near the eastern end of the Santa Fe Trail. Franklin was first used as the departure point, but when the Missouri River washed the community away in 1828, Independence quickly took its place. Then, Westport Landing, a suburb of today's Kansas City, succeeded Independence a few years later. From one of these towns, wagons plodded westward until they reached Council Grove, located nearly 150 miles out in the Kansas prairie. At the Grove, freighters organized their wagons into trains that consisted of around twenty-five vehicles each.

The organization of a wagon train was much like that of an army unit. Captains, lieutenants, and sergeants were elected by the wagons'

Westport Landing. WILLIAM H. JACKSON / PUBLIC DOMAIN

owners, and these officials' jobs were to command the entire train, with the clear understanding that their orders applied to everyone. US Army captain Randolph B. Marcy, the author of a popular traveler's guidebook of the period, described a typical wagon train's organization and the proper selection of its captain. He wrote:

> [T]heir first business should be to organise themselves into a company and elect a commander. The company should be of sufficient magnitude to herd and guard animals, and for protection against Indians. . . . From 50 to 70 men, properly armed and equipped, will be enough for these purposes, and any greater number makes the movements of the party more cumbersome and tardy. . . . In the selection of a captain, good judgment, integrity of purpose, and practical experience are the essential requisites. . . .
>
> His duty should be to direct the order of march, the time of starting and halting, to select the camps, detail and give orders to guards, and, indeed, to control and superintend all the moves of the company. . . . When a captain has been chosen, he should be sustained in all his

decisions unless he commits some manifest outrage, when a majority of the company can always remove him, and put a more competent man in his place.[1]

In order to protect the wagons, their owners, and their valuable contents, the entire male population of the train was divided up into watches. Each watch, consisting of several men, served for one-fourth of the night, every other night. Each man furnished his own weapon, whether it be rifle, pistol, or shotgun. Commenting on the armament of his own wagon train during his first trip across the Santa Fe Trail, Josiah Gregg wrote that "the party made altogether a very brigand-like appearance."[2]

When the wagon train left Council Grove, it was a well-organized unit, with a single purpose in mind—to get to Santa Fe as rapidly and as safely as possible.

A typical day on the Trail consisted of getting an early start while the morning was still cool. The teams were hitched and started on their way, each wagon commanded by either a bullwhacker, if oxen pulled, or by a mule skinner, if mules were used. These men kept the ten or twelve animals that pulled each wagon in line, since each pair of animals had

Wagons arriving at Santa Fe. FROM *COMMERCE OF THE PRAIRIES* / PUBLIC DOMAIN

their own job to perform, whether it was leading the others, doing heavy pulling, or initiating turns.

At around ten o'clock in the morning, a halt was called for the animals to rest and feed and for the men to eat breakfast, usually the biggest meal of the day. Equipment was repaired, the men might go hunting for game to add to the cooking pot, or they might just catch up on their sleep. At two o'clock in the afternoon, the teams were hitched back up, and the entire wagon train hit the trail again. Usually, three or four hours of steady travel was performed before the wagons stopped for the night at around five or six o'clock. In extremely hot weather, more travel was usually done at night and less in the daytime.

The freighters' reward came when they finally reached the fabled city of Santa Fe. After nearly two months of sleeping on the ground, eating less than favorable food, and breathing dust, the men were ready for the joys and vices that the ancient town offered. Josiah Gregg described a typical wagon train's arrival in his book, *Commerce of the Prairies*:

> *The arrival produced a great deal of bustle and excitement among the natives. "Los Americanos!"—"Los carros!"—"La entrada de la caravana!" were to be heard in every direction; and crowds of women and boys flocked around to see the newcomers. . . . The wagoners were by no means free from excitement on this occasion. Informed of the "ordeal" they had to pass, they had spent the previous morning in "rubbing up"; and now they were prepared, with clean faces, sleek combed hair, and their choicest Sunday suit, to meet the "fair eyes" of glistening black that were sure to stare at them as they passed. There was yet another preparation to be made in order to "show off" to advantage. Each wagoner must tie a brand new "cracker" to the lash of his whip; for, on driving through the streets and the plaza publica, every one strives to outvie his comrades in the dexterity with which he flourishes this favorite badge of authority.*[3]

All in all, a freighter's life was a hard one. If he personally owned his wagon and the goods that he carried in it, he was sure to realize a handsome profit at the end of the journey. But for the men and boys who just worked as bullwhackers, mule skinners, or herdsmen caring for the extra oxen and mules that usually accompanied the wagons, their days on the Santa Fe Trail were filled with hard work, heat, thirst, and very little pay.

Freighting was the primary business of the Santa Fe Trail. Whereas other American highways served as pathways for emigrants to search out new homes in the frontier wilderness (the Wilderness Road and the Oregon Trail), or provided the means to return home after extended business trips (the Natchez Trace), or simply offered the inhabitants of a new territory the convenience of easy travel between towns (the National Road), the Santa Fe Trail was a highway of empire, developed primarily for merchants seeking their fortunes in a far-off land. And so it continued for nearly fifty years until technology caught up with it in the form of the steam locomotive.

CHAPTER SIX

The First Military Escort
on the Santa Fe Trail

THE YEAR 1828 WAS NOT A GOOD ONE FOR SANTA FE TRADERS. IT HAD
started off well enough, and two large caravans made the journey from
Missouri to Santa Fe without incident. On the return trip, however, both
parties ran into difficulties with Indians. It all began when two young
traders, Daniel Munroe and a man named McNees, foolishly went to
sleep on the prairie some miles ahead of the main caravan. They were
attacked by a passerby Indian, or Indians, and shot with their own rifles.
McNees died immediately and Munroe sometime later. Josiah Gregg, in
his book, *Commerce of the Prairies*, writes what happened next:

> *Just as the funeral ceremonies were about to be concluded, six or seven
> Indians appeared on the opposite side of the Cimarron. Some of the
> party proposed inviting them to a parley, while the rest, burning for
> revenge, evinced a desire to fire upon them at once. It is more probable,
> however, that the Indians were not only innocent but ignorant of the
> outrage that had been committed, or they would hardly have ventured
> to approach the caravan. Being quick of perception, they very soon saw
> the belligerent attitude assumed by some of the company, and therefore
> wheeled round and attempted to escape. One shot was fired, which
> wounded a horse and brought the Indian to the ground, when he was
> instantly riddled with balls! Almost simultaneously another discharge
> of several guns followed, by which all the rest were either killed or*

mortally wounded, except one, who escaped to bear to his tribe the news of their dreadful catastrophe![1]

The subsequent ordeal of the traders was terrible. The Indians—apparently those whose kinsmen were slaughtered by the Americans—attacked the wagon trains with a fury. By the time the weary traders arrived back home, they had lost 1,000 head of horses and mules, $30,000 worth of profits, several wagons full of supplies, and three men.

But Indians had always, to one degree or another, posed problems for the Missouri traders. As early as 1824, when Thomas Hart Benton—who at the time was the chairman of the US Senate Committee on Indian Affairs—questioned a United States Indian agent about conditions along the Santa Fe Trail, the response was:

If the parties, trading to Santa Fé were less liable to interruption in their trade by the depredations of the different Indian tribes through which they are compelled to pass, I believe the trade would be carried on to a greater extent. . . . The Camanches [sic], Arrepahas [sic], Pawnees, and Osages, all cross the Santa Fé trail in their hunting or war parties; consequently, are liable to fall in with parties going to or coming from Santa Fé, and are very apt to steal their horses. . . . The chiefs say it is impossible for them to keep their young men from stealing from those parties.[2]

The disaster of 1828 on the heretofore relatively peaceful Santa Fe Trail caused an immediate outcry among the citizens of Missouri. Governor John Miller pointed an accusing finger at the national government for its absence of support for the fledgling Santa Fe trade. The Missouri Legislature called upon Congress to build a long-promised post at the Arkansas River crossing of the Trail, and at the same time, to furnish military escorts for the Missouri traders who made the long trip back and forth to Santa Fe. Senator Benton introduced a bill in the US Senate that would have provided such protection, but it never got out of committee hearings.

Just when it appeared that no real help was forthcoming from Washington, the Fayette, Missouri, newspaper of April 18, 1829, carried a front-page notice by Brigadier General Henry Atkinson that assistance was on the way. Major Bennet Riley, with two hundred men of the 6th US Infantry Regiment, would be leaving Cantonment Leavenworth around June 1, with explicit orders to escort Missouri traders across the Santa Fe Trail as far as the United States border with Mexico. The detachment of infantry would wait there until the return of the caravans in the fall and accompany them back to Missouri.

Major Riley and Companies A, B, F, and H arrived at Cantonment Leavenworth on May 15, 1829, aboard the steamboat *Diana*. The boat

Bennet Riley. L. G. SELLSTEDT, COURTESY OF THE US CAVALRY MUSEUM, FORT RILEY, KANSAS

had made the trip up the Missouri River from Jefferson Barracks, near St. Louis, in ten days. As it pulled up to the wharf at Leavenworth, it and its passengers were greeted with a fifteen-gun salute. The officers and men of the 6th Regiment now had less than a month to rest and to get their equipment in order for the long trip across the southern prairie to the Mexican border.

Riley and his command left Leavenworth on June 4, and by June 11 they had caught up with the trading party bound for Santa Fe at Round Grove, a few miles out in the Kansas prairie from Independence. Accompanying Riley was a six-pounder cannon, drawn by a mule, and twenty-four supply wagons and carts, pulled by oxen, the first time these animals had ever been employed on the Santa Fe Trail. As it turned out, one of the most important contributions made by Riley on this trip—aside, of course, from the protection that he provided the traders—was his proof that oxen were capable of pulling heavy loads across the Trail, a fact that was all the more relevant since oxen were much less expensive than mules.

Charles Bent, a man whose name would soon become indelibly linked with the Santa Fe Trail, was named captain of the seventy-man wagon caravan that left Round Grove the next day, following the infantrymen. By June 18 Riley's men and equipment, as well as the traders and their wagons, had reached Council Grove, the last vestige of American civilization along the Santa Fe Trail. Beyond this point, hostile Indians abounded, and danger lurked everywhere for the unwary. Council Grove also marked the last stop on the way to Santa Fe that hardwood for wagon axles could be cut. Consequently, Bent's caravan spent a day at the Grove making sure that all of the vehicles were in tip-top shape.

On June 20, the large group of soldiers and civilians left Council Grove and steered for the upper Arkansas Crossing of the Santa Fe Trail, located near Chouteau's Island. The trip during the next three weeks was uneventful, and on July 9 the wagon caravan and its military escort arrived at the island, situated in the Arkansas River. Here, the stream served as the dividing line between Mexican and United States territory. This was the point designated by the army where Major Riley and his infantrymen would leave the traders on their own. The soldiers would bivouac in the area until October 10, which was the latest date agreed upon for Bent's trading party to arrive back at the boundary line for its rendezvous with Major Riley and the escort back to Missouri.

Bent's Missouri traders were happy that they had made it this far without a mishap or a serious confrontation with Indians. On July 10, the thankful members of the caravan presented Major Riley with a memorial, which read:

> *Resolved That the thanks of the Company be presented to Major Bennet Riley and through him to the Officers and Soldiers under his command for the effectual protection and generous assistance they have given us on a march through a Savage Wilderness of nearly five hundred miles during . . . which nothing has been wanting on their part that energy and preseverance [sic] could overcome.*[3]

On the same day, Riley sent a letter to the Mexican governor at Santa Fe. The major advised the official that he had safely arrived at the international border. He also requested—since reports had been received that Indians had caused considerable depredation on both sides of the border—that the Mexican government provide an armed escort for Bent's caravan while the American traders traveled across its territory.

The river crossing was made the next day, and the wagon train slowly made its way southward. The part of the Santa Fe Trail that it now traveled, the Cimarron Cutoff, dissected a desolate desert wilderness where sources for water were practically nonexistent. And, it was an ideal spot for Indian attacks, since weary travelers were habitually distracted from their surroundings while simply trying to survive the heat and drought.

Only a few miles separated the caravan from its escort when the traders were fallen upon by a band of Kiowa Indians. One freighter was immediately killed in the ambush, and Charles Bent quickly issued orders to corral the wagons and dig rifle pits. A small cannon that the traders carried with them was swung into action, and Bent dispatched nine volunteers back to the Arkansas to fetch Major Riley and his men.

Although it was clearly understood by all parties concerned that Riley's escort was, under no circumstances, to cross the Arkansas River into Mexican territory, the messengers from Bent left the major with little choice. He quickly assembled his infantrymen and marched them on the double to the rescue. To the American soldiers unfamiliar with the heat and severe drought of the region, the journey to and from Bent's relief was almost intolerable. Lieutenant Philip St. George Cooke wrote of the experience later:

> *Emerging from the hills, we found ourselves on the verge of a vast plain, nearly level, where it seemed nature had ineffectually struggled to convert a sandy desert into a prairie. There was a scanty and dwarfish growth of wiry grass, brown and withered, amid the white sand. On we marched, under a fiery sun, facing a burning wind. Not a tree, not a shrub, not the slightest indication of water could be seen in a view apparently illimitable in every direction. Thus we struggled on until noon, when the panting oxen, with lolling tongues, seemed incapable of proceeding.*[4]

Riley's men pulled into the besieged camp of the traders at one o'clock on the morning of July 11. Ideally, their arrival should have been kept a secret, but when a bugler blew reveille at daybreak, the frightened Indians, now realizing that the army had arrived, lifted the siege and left the area. The soldiers escorted the wagon train for a few more miles into the scorching desert before Riley, on July 13, decided that his men had penetrated Mexican territory far enough. On the same day, Charles Bent wrote a letter to Major Riley requesting that his men accompany the caravan all the way to Santa Fe. Bent pleaded:

> *At once to come boldly to the point, we solicit your further protection though well knowing it is against your positive order, nothing can induce us to make this request but the pressing dangers which surround us & of which you are duly apprized. But to support us in this solicitation we beg leave to remark, that extraordinary cases do sometimes occur upon which no law rule or order will bear they are so*

*portentous that instructions cannot apply to them. . . . As we are fully
apprized of the responsibility of your situation; we will not ask for
too much. We are induced to believe that twenty or thirty men would
insure our safety if they were permitted to proceed to the Red River
. . . this side of Santa Fe.*[5]

On the following day, Major Riley regretfully declined Bent's request.
He replied:

*Gentlemen, there is nothing that would give me more pleasure than
to accompany you through to the end of your dangerous journey. But
. . . it is impossible; in the first place my teams are nearly given out for
want of food. . . . In the second place I know that if I was to attempt
to accompany you through, I would be obliged to leave my Waggons
in the Prairie and we ourselves to leave you even before we could get
near Santa Fe. . . . Gentlemen, it is not the fear of the disapprobation
of my Government that prevents me from accompanying you . . . but
the fear that my Teams would give out on the road. . . . I hope you will
not think hard when I have to tell you again, that it is impossible for
me to go any farther with you.*[6]

On July 15 Riley's command turned back toward the American border.

Left alone once again, the Missouri traders continued toward Santa
Fe. Somewhere along the way, a Mexican escort of 120 men joined the
Americans, but the Indians continued to attack the wagons in a hit-and-
run fashion. Ewing Young, a Tennessee-born fur trapper who operated
out of Taos, heard about the train's predicament and recruited more than
ninety fellow trappers from the area and soon rendezvoused with the
wagons. With the new reinforcements, Bent's wagons and men were able
to safely complete their journey to Santa Fe, by way of Taos.

In the meantime, Major Riley and his infantrymen had returned to
the United States border and established a camp along the north bank of
the Arkansas River, near Chouteau's Island, to await the autumn return
of Captain Bent's caravan. On July 31 four soldiers in Riley's command,

whose enlistments were up, started for home. Several miles east of camp, Indians approached and killed one of the men. A hunting party from Riley's encampment rescued the other three soldiers later in the day.

On August 3 some three hundred to four hundred Indians, supposedly Comanche and Kiowa, attacked Major Riley's camp. One soldier was mortally wounded while he guarded the stock, but eight Indians were also killed during the forty-five-minute skirmish. Before they retreated, the Indians stole fifty oxen and twenty horses and mules, and disabled several other animals.

All was relatively quiet around the army camp until August 11, when a detail of infantrymen was sent out to bring in three buffalo that had been shot by hunters earlier in the day. The party was surrounded by about 150 Indians, and the bugler was shot and scalped before Riley could send out reinforcements to the rescue.

After these several encounters, the Indians appeared to leave the region. It was also after these incidents with the war parties that Riley's second important contribution was made. It was his realization of the futility of foot soldiers trying to keep the peace with mounted Indians. In his official report, Riley wrote that his men's feelings were dashed as they watched the enemy ride off with the large number of cattle and horses,

Riley's escort of Charles Bent's caravan. COURTESY OF JAMES A. CRUTCHFIELD

whereas if the soldiers had been likewise mounted, they could have given chase and recovered the animals.

The days of late August and September passed slowly while the nervous infantrymen tried to relax, or hunted buffalo, or simply looked forward to the days when they would be back home with family and friends. However, the need for vigilance was always present. Lieutenant Cooke described the importance of staying alert in the event of an Indian attack when he wrote that he was:

> *Officer of the guard every fourth night. I was always awake, and generally in motion the whole night. Night alarms were frequent; when, all sleeping in their clothes, we were accustomed to assemble instantly, and with scarcely a word spoken, take our places in the grass in front of each face of the camp, where, however wet, we sometimes lay for hours. I never failed . . . to sleep in pantaloons and moccasins, with pistols, and a loose woolen coat for pillow; my sword stuck in the ground in the mouth of the tent, with my cap upon the hilt; and although I have often slept undisturbed at the firing of a cannon thirty paces off, here, always after the firing of a musket, if 500 paces off, in less than ten seconds I was out and ready to perform my duty.*[7]

As October 10 approached—the last day agreed upon for the trading caravan to cross back over the American border to take advantage of the army escort—Riley's men made preparations for the long march east.

October 10 arrived and passed and the American traders were nowhere in sight. The following day, Riley and his command struck camp and started for Cantonment Leavenworth. Unbeknownst to the major, Bent's traders were only about twenty miles from the American border. They had left Santa Fe on September 1, and their caravan, in addition to the Missourians and about thirty wagons, now consisted of sixteen Spanish refugees; two thousand horses, mules, and jackasses; and two hundred Mexican soldiers who rode as escorts under the command of Colonel José Antonio Vizcarra.

Bent, apprehensive that the rendezvous with the army escort would not be made on time, sent messengers ahead to locate Riley's command, which had scarcely marched three miles from camp when the courier caught up with them. Halting the march, Riley waited until the next day when the caravan and its Mexican escort approached. On October 14 the Missouri traders, along with Major Riley and the men of the 6th Infantry, left the wagon train's Mexican protectors and started for home. As they neared civilization, the traders and the escort party separated and went their own ways—the merchants to their Missouri homes, and Riley's men to Cantonment Leavenworth, where they arrived on November 8 amid another fifteen-gun salute.

Although the War Department would eventually provide protection for Santa Fe–bound wagon trains, during the several years immediately following Major Riley's adventures with the Bent train, the army declined to use its men to escort Missouri traders on their missions to New Mexico. The reasoning behind the decisions was the fact that, as Riley had pointed out, infantrymen were no match for mounted Indians, and, at the time, there were no comparable United States cavalry troops. Secondly, the region through which the escorts would have been allowed to travel were always the safest parts of the journey to Santa Fe; it was usually on the Mexican side of the Arkansas River—where the army had no authority and was ordered not to go—that the real danger from Indians arose.

The army's lack of immediate cooperation in offering escorts for Santa Fe–bound caravans resulted in the realization among the traders that if the wagon trains were going to be protected at all, it was up to the merchants themselves to provide such service. Accordingly, over the next few years, the personnel of the caravans were organized into more-disciplined and military-like units, and ones that could render their own protection against marauding Indians.

CHAPTER SEVEN

Bent's Fort

ONE OF THE SANTA FE TRAIL'S MOST NOTED LANDMARKS DURING ITS years as a highway of commerce linking the Missouri settlements and the villages of New Mexico was Bent's Fort, located near the present-day town of La Junta, Colorado.

Bent's Fort was built in 1833 by Charles and William Bent and Ceran St. Vrain. Charles, the oldest of the four famous Bent brothers, was born in Charleston, Virginia (now West Virginia), in 1799. When he was six years old, he moved to St. Louis with his mother and father, and there, in the town that served as the gateway to the West, he grew to manhood amid the sights and sounds of the trapper and trader communities.

While still a young man, Bent joined the Missouri Fur Company and spent considerable time on the upper Missouri River, although his exact position with the company is unknown. Poor success of the Missouri Fur Company caused young Bent to look in other directions for his future, and his sights soon became set on the newly opened Santa Fe trade. Convinced that the wave of the future pointed to the Southwest, Bent immersed himself in the New Mexican trade.

Charles Bent's younger brother, William, was born in St. Louis in 1809. By 1824 William, deeply influenced by Charles, was trapping along the upper reaches of the Arkansas River and was well familiar with the section of the southern Great Plains through which the Santa Fe Trail ran. The other partner in the construction of the post, Ceran St. Vrain, was of French descent and was born in Missouri in 1802. As early as 1825, St. Vrain was a frequent visitor to Taos in New Mexico.

In 1830 Charles Bent and Ceran St. Vrain organized Bent, St. Vrain & Company, soon to become the foundation for a commercial empire that covered thousands of square miles. When the company built the adobe fort for trading purposes, it was first known as Fort William, in honor of brother William, who supervised its construction. The name was later changed to Bent's Fort.

In time William became the major driving force in the day-to-day management of activities at Bent's Fort, and it was he who guided the company through its successful trading operations among the Indian tribes of the southern Great Plains. William married a Cheyenne Indian named Owl Woman and became even more Indian-like in his habits. His influence among the Cheyenne through his marriage to Owl Woman did a great deal to enhance the peace between various Plains tribes and the rapidly approaching whites. In the meantime, Charles Bent had established a permanent home in Taos, the small Mexican-Indian village north of Santa Fe. He married an affluent Mexican widow, and even though he retained his American citizenship, he involved himself in the business affairs of the town and soon became one of its leading citizens.

Within a few years of its construction, Bent's Fort became the hub for the extensive Bent, St. Vrain operations that reached into today's states of Wyoming, Utah, Colorado, New Mexico, Arizona, Texas, Oklahoma, Kansas, and Nebraska. The fort was a citadel in the wilderness and was frequented by mountain men, Missouri and Taos traders, Mexicans, and members of several tribes of Great Plains and Southwest Indians.

Bent's Fort was a magnificent structure built with adobe bricks. The compound measured 142 feet by 122 feet and contained twenty-six rooms that surrounded a small courtyard. Space was provided inside the fort for corrals, wagon sheds, and a blacksmith. Although it was built primarily as a trading post, the fort's strategic location hundreds of miles deep into Indian Territory made it necessary that it be able to serve as a defensive structure as well.

Massive walls, with two conical bastions perched on opposite corners, protected the living quarters, storehouses, and water well inside. A small cannon was placed in a watchtower above the walls, and an American flag

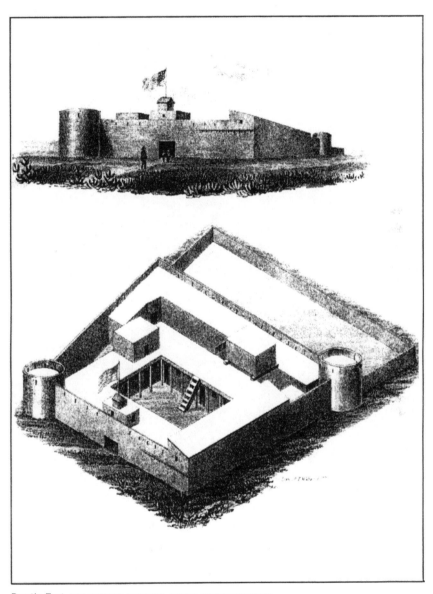

Bent's Fort. LIEUTENANT JAMES W. ABERT / PUBLIC DOMAIN

flew proudly from a flagstaff over the gate. A visitor of the time estimated that Bent's Fort could accommodate upward of one hundred men.

Matthew Field, a reporter for the New Orleans *Picayune*, visited Bent's Fort during the summer of 1839. The newspaperman left a poetic vision of how the adobe stronghold looked when he wrote:

> *Bricks moulded from the prairie clay*
> *And roasted in the noontide ray.*
> *Large as the stones of city halls*
> *From good "Fort William's" strong built walls.*
> *And trunks and boughs of "Cotton Wood"*
> *Form gates and beams and rafters good.*
> *While grass and mud piled closely o'er,*
> *Forms sheltering roof and sanded floor.*
> *A strong-barred gate, a rampart wall,*
> *And Bastions, guard the stock corral,*
> *And here some fifty inmates dwell*
> *From year to year content and well.*[1]

Fur press at Bent's Fort. COURTESY OF REGENA H. CRUTCHFIELD

George Frederick Ruxton, a young Englishman who journeyed throughout much of the American Southwest during the Mexican War, visited the fort in 1847 and left the following description in his book about his western travels:

Bent's Fort is situated on the left or northern bank of the river Arkansa [sic], about one hundred miles from the foot of the Rocky Mountains—on a low and level bluff of the prairie which here slopes gradually to the water's edge. The walls are built entirely of adobes—or sun-burned bricks—in the form of a hollow square, at two corners of which are circular flanking towers of the same material. The entrance is by a large gateway into the square, round which are the rooms occupied by traders and employees of the host. They are small in size, with walls coloured by a white-wash made of clay found in the prairie. Their flat roofs are defended along the exterior by parapets of adobe, to serve as a cover to marksmen firing from the top. . . . In the centre of the square is the press for packing the furs; and there are three large rooms, one used as a store and magazine, another as a council-room, where the Indians assemble for their "talks," whilst the third is the common dining-hall, where the traders, trappers, and hunters, and all employees, feast upon the best provender the game-covered country affords . . .

The appearance of the fort is very striking, standing as it does hundreds of miles from any settlement, on the vast and lifeless prairie, surrounded by hordes of hostile Indians, and far out of reach of intercourse with civilized man.[2]

Another first-person account of the fort, and one that more vividly describes its military attributes, is given by Lieutenant James W. Abert, a topographical engineer with Frémont's expedition of 1845. The following year, Abert accompanied Colonel Kearny's Army of the West from Fort Leavenworth as far as the post. In August 1845, Abert wrote:

The fort is composed of a series of rooms resembling casemates, and forming a hollow square, the entrance on the east side. A round tower on the left, as you enter, and another diagonally opposite, constitute the flanking arrangements. The outer walls, which are nearly two feet in thickness, intersect in the axes of the towers, thus permitting their faces to be completely enfiladed; the outside walls . . . and towers, pierced with loop holes, are continued four feet above the flat roofs which serve for the banquette, which being composed of clay cannot be fired by inflammable substances that might be cast upon it; the whole is built of "adobes," sunburnt brick, formed of clay and cut straw, in size about four times as large as our common bricks. The roofs are sustained by poles. On the west side is the cattle yard, which is surrounded by a wall so high as effectually to shelter them. The coping of the wall is planted with cacti, which bear red and white flowers.[3]

At any particular time, one might find mountain men, members of several of the southern Great Plains Indian tribes, Santa Fe traders, and US Army personnel, all gathered together at Bent's Fort. One of its primary attractions was the savory food served to weary travelers. The kitchen was supervised by Charlotte Green, the black servant of the Bent brothers, and a fine cook who was known all over the Southwest for her pancakes and pumpkin pie.

Bent's Fort reigned supreme on the Santa Fe Trail for many years. However, as more and more of the thoroughfare's wagon traffic began to travel the shorter, smoother Cimarron Cutoff route, and as trapping activity in the vicinity gradually came to a close, the old fort slowly lost its importance as a dominant factor in the Santa Fe trade. The remains of the post finally became a stop on the Kansas City, Denver, and Santa Fe stagecoach line that was operated by Barlow-Sanderson Overland Stage, Mail and Express Company, but not before William Bent and his family packed up their belongings and rode out of the gates, never to return. Some stories even say that Bent, disillusioned by the US Army's failure to pay him a fair price for the structure, deliberately blew up the fort when he deserted it.

CHAPTER EIGHT

Women on the Santa Fe Trail

THE FACT THAT THE SANTA FE TRAIL WAS PRIMARILY A HIGHWAY OF commerce made it reasonable that men frequented it more often than women. Some ladies, however, did make the long trip across the prairie with their families. It was a dusty, hot ordeal, but the women appear to have endured the hardships just as well as the men did.

The first documented Anglo-American woman to travel across the Santa Fe Trail was Mary Dodson Donoho. The twenty-six-year-old daughter of a prominent Tennessee, later Missouri, physician, Mary was accompanied by her husband, William, and the couple's nine-month-old daughter, Mary Ann. As the small family tossed about in their wagon on the final leg of the trek, they took some solace in knowing that nearly one hundred other vehicles—packed full with almost two hundred Missouri traders, supplies for the trip, and thousands of dollars' worth of trade goods for use at the end of the Trail—had journeyed across the hot, dry southern Great Plains with them.

The famed trader Charles Bent, who in 1846 would become the first American governor of New Mexico, was elected captain of the wagon train. Constant rains delayed the traders' departure from Council Grove until June 19, 1833. However, after the procession started rolling across the prairie, no additional serious difficulties were encountered. Just to be safe, though, part of the US 6th Infantry, under the command of Captain William N. Wickliffe, and a field cannon accompanied Captain Bent's goods-laden wagons. On July 11, the day after the caravan crossed the Arkansas River, which constituted the boundary between the United States and Mexico, the military escort returned to Fort Leavenworth.

At last, the noisy, lumbering wagons entered the town of Santa Fe, clamored down the narrow street that led to the Plaza, crossed the nearly dry Santa Fe River, and arrived at the Palace of the Governors. Although the Donohos left no written record of their impressions of the town, another resident, Francisco Perea, described the capital of New Mexico in 1837–1838 as

> *full of soldiers, citizens, and a miscellaneous gathering of humanity of all stations of life, the plaza being crowded with all kinds of vehicles, beginning with the cart that was made entirely of wood . . . to the well-constructed wagon that had brought a consignment of merchandise over the Santa Fe Trail; together with teamsters, camp-cooks, roustabouts, horses, mules, burros, pigs, and goats. Some were about their camp-fires preparing their food, while others were feeding and caring for their animals.*[1]

History has not revealed just exactly why William Donoho wanted to leave his relatively affluent life in Missouri and travel the long distance to Santa Fe. What is even more intriguing is why he carried his wife and infant daughter on the trip, unless he fully intended to settle there and make the sleepy New Mexican town his permanent home. Otherwise, he, like all the rest of the traders, would simply have disposed of his trade goods in Santa Fe and returned to his home in Boone County, Missouri, for the winter.

It must be assumed then, that the Donohos planned on settling in Santa Fe, and their subsequent activities seem to bear this out. The couple went into the hotel business, and within a short time after their arrival in town, they opened a hostelry on the southeast corner of the Plaza on the site of today's renowned La Fonda. According to local tradition, a hotel had stood on that very corner since Santa Fe was originally settled. No doubt with the rapid increase in the number of

American traders who journeyed to the town every summer, William and Mary must have decided that the hotel business would be as profitable to pursue as any.

Again, the Donohos left no record of what their establishment was like, but if it was similar to the other hotels in town, as described by Francisco Perea, it was:

of a very primitive kind, where travelers and others could obtain meals and lodging, and also shelter and feed the horses and other animals. The food was wholly prepared after the Mexican customs, and the favorite dish of chili, prepared in one way or another, was seldom absent from the menu. Native wine was served at the table when desired. The beds were scrupulously clean and in every way inviting for repose. Fireplaces built into the adobe walls were used for both heating and cooking purposes, there being no stoves of any sort at that time. Rates for the entertainment of transient, as well as local, guests were very reasonable, and the conventional amenities of the hostelers in the entertainment of their guests was without fault.[2]

The Donohos operated their hotel on the Plaza for nearly four years, when heightened danger accompanying a revolt against Governor Albino Perez caused concern about the safety of the family. In late August or early September 1837, William, Mary, Mary Ann, and two other children—Harriet and James, the first Anglo-American girl and boy born in New Mexico—made the long trip back to Missouri.

During his stay in Santa Fe, William was instrumental in rescuing three women—Sarah Ann Horn, Rachael Plummer, and a Mrs. Harris—from Comanche captivity, and supervised the return of all three to Missouri. The journey of the three women over the Santa Fe Trail may have been the second instance of Anglo women traveling the thoroughfare. Mary Donoho assisted her husband in this noble effort, and Mrs. Plummer, in her book recalling the ordeal, later wrote:

I have no language to express my gratitude to Mrs. Donoho. I found in her a mother . . . a sister . . . a friend . . . one who was continually pouring the sweet oil of consolation into my wounded and trembling soul.[3]

Sarah Ann Horn, a young Englishwoman who had traveled with her family to distant Texas to settle the unexplored land there, was equally complimentary of the Donohos. The couple had retrieved her from certain death following her husband's murder by the Comanche and her own separation from her children. In Horn's narrative, she wrote:

[S]hall I never forget, that when the angry billows of life's stormy sea, lashed into fury by misfortune's awful frown, had thrown me a trembling victim upon their coast, the American traders took me up—they bound up my wounds—they spake comfortably to me, while their countenance reflected the mild and heavenly beams of the angel of mercy.[4]

In later years, the Donoho family again pulled up stakes in Missouri and moved to Clarksville, Texas, where they operated the Donoho Hotel, a place that was renowned throughout the region for its hospitality and fine food and accommodations. William Donoho died in Clarksville in September 1845. Mary survived, a well-respected and affluent member of the Clarksville community, until she passed away quietly, "without previous illness," in January 1880.

In June 1846 the next American woman of whom there is a record left Independence, Missouri, for Santa Fe. She was Susan Shelby Magoffin, the granddaughter of the first governor of Kentucky, Isaac Shelby. Susan and her husband, Samuel, a well-known trader, arrived in Santa Fe just two weeks after the American army under General Stephen Watts Kearny occupied the town. Later, Susan left Santa Fe and traveled down into Mexico, visiting along the way the towns of El Paso, Chihuahua, and Saltillo. Her child was born in Mexico, but died soon after birth. Susan returned to Kentucky shortly thereafter.

NARRATIVE

OF THE

CAPTIVITY OF MRS. HORN,

AND HER TWO CHILDREN,

WITH

MRS. HARRIS,

BY THE

CAMANCHE INDIANS,

AFTER THEY HAD MURDERED THEIR HUSBANDS AND TRAVELLING COMPANIONS;

WITH A BRIEF ACCOUNT OF THE

Manners and Customs of that Nation of Savages,

OF WHOM SO LITTLE IS GENERALLY KNOWN.

> Time and distance might efface,
> To some extent, the ill that's past;
> But while she weeps her *captive* boy,
> Her bitterest cup of woe shall last.

COPYRIGHT SECURED.

ST. LOUIS:

C. KEEMLE, PRINTER, 22 OLIVE ST.

1839.

Title page of Sarah Ann Horn's book. FROM *NARRATIVE OF THE CAPTIVITY OF MRS. HORN, AND HER TWO CHILDREN, WITH MRS. HARRIS, BY THE CAMANCHE INDIANS* / COURTESY OF JAMES A. CRUTCHFIELD

Wagons negotiating Raton Pass. COURTESY OF JAMES A. CRUTCHFIELD

Fortunately, for future generations of historians, Susan Magoffin left a detailed diary of her day-to-day activities as she traveled along the Santa Fe Trail. Reading the journal today makes one aware of the multitude of hardships that were experienced by those early travelers across the southern prairie. The Magoffins had barely left Independence when Susan described a typical camp scene:

> [T]he hot sun, or rather the wind which blew pretty roughly, compelled me to seek shelter with my friends, the carriage & a thick veil. . . . The animals made an extensive show indeed. Mules and oxen scattered in all directions. The teamsters were just "catching up," and the cracking of whips, lowing of cattle, braying of mules, whooping and hallowing of the men, was a novel sight.[5]

Susan spent her nineteenth birthday at Bent's Fort, but it appears that it was just another day for the young Kentucky woman. She wrote:

> There is the greatest possible noise in the patio. The shoeing of horses, neighing, and braying of mules, the crying of children, the scolding and fighting of men, are all enough to turn my head. And to add to the scene, like some of our neighbors we have our own private troubles. The servants are all quarreling and fighting among themselves, running to us to settle their difficulties; they are gambling . . . and though each of them are in debt . . . they are coming [to us] . . . to get them out of their scrapes.[6]

After leaving Bent's Fort, Susan and her party neared Raton Pass, on the border of today's states of Colorado and New Mexico. The mountains here were high, and the wagon train had to climb carefully through the rocky precipices that lined the pass through the mountains. An exasperated and tired Susan wrote:

> Worse and worse the road! They are even taking the mules from the carriages this P.M. and a half dozen men by bodily exertions are pulling them down the hills. And it takes a dozen men to steady a wagon with all its wheels locked—and for one who is some distance

off to hear the crash it makes over the stones, is truly alarming. Till I rode ahead and understood the business, I supposed that every wagon had fallen over a precipice. We came to camp about half an hour after dusk, having accomplished the great travel of six or eight hundred yards during the day.[7]

When the wagon train at last reached Santa Fe, Susan and her husband were happy indeed.

It is really hard to realize it, that I am here in my own house, in a place to where I once would have thought it folly to think of visiting. I have entered the city in a year that will always be remembered by my countrymen; and under the "Star-spangled banner" too.[8]

Susan and her husband stayed in Santa Fe for some time before beginning the remainder of their trip that would carry them southward into Mexico, and finally, back to the United States. Susan was an observant tourist, and her diary is full of descriptions of the sights and the scenes that she experienced during her travels. One of her favorite spots in Santa Fe was the Plaza, alongside which, several years earlier, Mary and William Donoho had operated their hotel. Susan later wrote:

The plazo [sic] or square is very large—on one side is the government house with a wide portal in front, opposite is a large church commenced by the predecessor of Gov. Armijo, 'tis not finished—and dwelling houses—the two remaining sides are fronted with stores and dwellings, all with portals, a shed the width of our pavements; it makes a fine walk—and in rainy weather there is no use for an umbrella.[9]

After Susan Magoffin, several other American women and girls journeyed down the Santa Fe Trail. Two who left records were Marian Mahoney Russell and Ernestine Huning. Seven-year-old Marian, along with her mother and brother, left Westport Landing in 1852, bound for California. After reaching Santa Fe, the family's money was stolen, so plans for going on to the Pacific Coast were dropped. The Mahoneys moved back

East four years later, but in 1860, the threesome returned once again to Santa Fe. In 1865 Marian married Lieutenant Richard Russell at Fort Union on the Santa Fe Trail. Afterward, when her husband was away on assignment, Marion stayed at Fort Larned, in Kansas, also along the Trail. Mrs. Russell lived until 1936.

German-born Ernestine Huning traveled the Santa Fe Trail in 1863 with her new husband, Franz, who had already established himself in Albuquerque as a successful hardware dealer. Four years later, when Franz was bringing Ernestine's mother and brother over the Trail to New Mexico from Missouri, his wagon train was attacked by Indians. The outcome was disastrous. Franz wrote to his wife on September 10, 1867:

> *Yesterday afternoon we were attacked by Indians and Fritz was badly wounded. The Mother had been quite weak for several days so that the shock and grief of seeing her son in such a critical condition has made her so weak, causing heart trouble, that the doctor does not think she can last through the day. She is conscious only part of the time, and then she tells me what to say to you, and that she must die. Regarding Fritz the doctor tells me one time that he cannot live and then that he may recover. He was wounded in the chest. My opinion is that his condition is hopeless; be prepared for the worst.*[10]

Two days later Franz wrote to Ernestine again and sadly reported that her mother had died. "She told me at the last that she would have liked to see you once more, but as it was not God's will, she would die content, knowing that you are well cared for,"[11] he wrote. The following day, Franz again wrote to Ernestine, this time informing her of her brother's death. He lamented, "Knowing that his Mother was dead he said he would die satisfied. . . . United as they were in life, I had them buried side by side."[12]

No doubt over the years, other women and girls, for whom no documentation has yet been discovered, made the long trip between Missouri and Santa Fe along the Trail. It was a long, tortuous, dangerous journey, but in the end, most of these hardy women persevered to bring American culture and lifestyles to the remote villages and towns of New Mexico.

CHAPTER NINE

Josiah Gregg

WILLIAM BECKNELL'S NAME IS USUALLY ASSOCIATED WITH THE SANTA Fe Trail because of his early trading exploits with the inhabitants of New Mexico. However, it remained for another man to document the life and times of the Trail. Josiah Gregg, in his book *Commerce of the Prairies*, published in New York in 1844, has left future generations with a classic account of his life as a trader in Santa Fe. The book is also a gold mine of information about the Trail itself, as well as the geography, geology, and ethnology of the region through which it passes. Indeed, the subtitle of Gregg's masterpiece, *The Journal of a Santa Fe Trader During Eight Expeditions Across the Great Western Prairies, and a Residence of Nearly Nine Years in Northern Mexico*, describes the contents very well.

Josiah Gregg was born in 1806 in Tennessee, the son of a wheelwright who moved frequently from place to place. By the time Josiah was eight years old, he was living at the edge of the Western frontier in Missouri. Young Gregg was a sickly lad, and indeed, there was doubt that he would live to see manhood. But the boy endured and grew up to become an intelligent, well-educated man, disciplined in mathematics, surveying, and literature.

Around the year 1830, Gregg became ill again. He had always been a consumptive-type person, but exactly what this later illness was has never been determined. He was studying law at the time, and perhaps the pressures of his concentration, coupled with his predisposition toward illness, became too much for him. In any event, his physician advised him to take the next wagon train to Santa Fe. He did, and thus began Josiah Gregg's romance with the American Southwest and the Santa Fe Trail.

Gregg's relocation must have temporarily cured him, because between 1831 and 1840, he made eight trips across the southern Great Plains on the Santa Fe Trail. During some of his journeys, he spent several months at a time in Santa Fe, which he came to know and love as much as any town he had ever visited.

An early description of Santa Fe as it appeared to Americans during the height of the greatest trading period of the 1830s is given by Gregg in his book.

> *Santa Fe, the capital of New Mexico, is the only town of any importance in the province. . . . Like most of the towns in this section of country it occupies the site of an ancient Pueblo or Indian village. . . . The population of the city itself but little exceeds 3,000, yet, including several surrounding villages which are embraced in its corporate jurisdiction, it amounts to nearly 6,000 souls. The town is very irregularly laid out, and most of the streets are little better than common highways traversing scattered settlements which are interspersed with cornfields.*[1]

Drawing upon his training in medicine, which he had received as a young man while living in Kentucky, Gregg practiced his art among the poor inhabitants of New Mexico. But his real love was in the recording of every event, every strange sight, every peculiar sound that he witnessed. With a keen eye for observation, young Gregg, in his *Commerce of the Prairies*, gives the reader as complete a study of the Santa Fe Trail and its surroundings as could ever be hoped for.

Gregg was one of the first writers to recognize the importance of the bison to the economy of many American Indian tribes, as pointed out in his quotation in chapter 1 of this book. He was also among the first to understand that the continued killing of the bison for sport and hides would eventually lead to the species' extinction. He wrote:

> *Were they only killed for food, however, their natural increase would perhaps replenish the loss: yet the continual and wanton slaughter*

*of them by travelers and hunters, and the still greater havoc made
among them by the Indians, not only for meat, but often for the skins
and tongues alone (for which they find a ready market among their
traders), are fast reducing their numbers, and must ultimately effect
their total annihilation from the continent.*[2]

Although he had quit the Santa Fe trade by 1843, the year he began
preparing his book for publication, Gregg told of one event that had
occurred earlier in the year that almost caused an international incident.
The trouble started two years before when a group of Texans marched on
Santa Fe hoping to persuade its citizens to join the Republic of Texas.

Josiah Gregg. COURTESY OF JAMES A. CRUTCHFIELD

COMMERCE OF THE PRAIRIES:

OR THE

Journal of a Santa Fé Trader,

DURING

EIGHT EXPEDITIONS ACROSS

THE GREAT WESTERN PRAIRIES,

AND

A RESIDENCE OF NEARLY NINE YEARS

IN

NORTHERN MEXICO.

Illustrated with Maps and Engravings.

BY JOSIAH GREGG.

IN TWO VOLUMES.

VOL. I.

NEW YORK:

HENRY G. LANGLEY, 8 ASTOR HOUSE.

M DCCC XLIV.

Title page of Josiah Gregg's book. FROM *COMMERCE OF THE PRAIRIES* / PUBLIC DOMAIN

The mission failed miserably when most of the participants were arrested by Mexican authorities.

Friends and relatives of the expedition's members back in Texas called for revenge. Accordingly, several Texans decided to take matters into their own hands and do something about the embarrassing defeat their kinsman had suffered at the hands of the Mexican governor. Several gangs of ruffians began to ride back and forth across the southern Great Plains, their object being to attack any eastbound wagon trains driven by Mexicans. The threat posed by the Texans did not appear to bother Antonio José Chávez, a well-to-do Santa Fe merchant. He left New Mexico for Missouri in February 1843, accompanied by five servants, two wagons, and fifty-five mules. He carried with him about ten to twelve thousand dollars' worth of gold bullion.

By April 10 Chávez and his party were more than one hundred miles inside the United States border. There he was captured by the ruffians. Josiah Gregg continues the story:

> *The unfortunate Mexican was . . . taken a few miles south of the road, and his baggage rifled. Seven of the party then left . . . with their share of the booty, amounting to some four or five hundred dollars apiece. . . . The remaining eight, soon after the departure of their comrades, determined to put Chávez to death,—for what cause it would seem difficult to conjecture, as he had been, for two days, their unresisting prisoner. Lots were cast to determine which four of the party would be the cruel executioners; and their wretched victim was taken off a few rods and shot down in cold blood.*[3]

The senseless murder raised the ire of Mexicans and Americans alike, and most of the culprits were caught and brought to justice. The illegal raiding forays along the Santa Fe Trail ended when Captain Philip St. George Cooke of the US Army and two hundred dragoons faced down the Texans a short time after the Chávez affair.

Josiah Gregg traveled the Santa Fe Trail so many times that he was well qualified to describe the best camping places along the route, and to give distances between them. He reported in his book that the total mileage from Independence, Missouri, to Santa Fe was 775 miles; from Council Grove, where the individual wagons were usually organized into trains, the distance was 625 miles to Santa Fe. Both of these routes were measured along the shorter Cimarron Cutoff.[4]

Gregg's book is also important because it gives figures about the yearly traffic along the Trail. In one particularly interesting part, he describes the number of wagons and men who traveled the Trail for the years between 1822 and 1843, as well as the value of the merchandise for those years.[5] Chapters on mining, New Mexican government, Indians, agriculture, wildlife, and history, among other subjects, make Gregg's *Commerce of the Prairies* one of the most important books ever written about the Santa Fe Trail.

Gregg eventually left the Santa Fe trade to pursue other interests. During the Mexican War, he served as a newspaper correspondent, and later, he emigrated to the California goldfields. In February 1850, when he was only forty-four years old, he fell from his horse and was mortally injured. Today, his body lies at the spot of his death, near Clear Lake, California.

William Becknell did much, indeed, to make the Santa Fe Trail the highway of commerce that it quickly became after his first successful trips to New Mexico in 1821 and 1822. Josiah Gregg, however, through the magic of the written word, brought the romance and mystery of the Trail to anyone who would take the time to read his wonderful book.

CHAPTER TEN

The Army of the West

ALTHOUGH THE SANTA FE TRAIL WAS PRIMARILY A HIGHWAY FOR traders, the largest assemblage of men and animals ever to travel the thoroughfare had absolutely nothing to do with commerce. That honor goes to the US Army in 1846, when it ordered a large military contingent to New Mexico and California. In May 1846, war broke out between the United States and Mexico over the Texas annexation issue. Texas, which had been an independent republic since its separation from Mexico in 1836, was added to the United States by President James K. Polk in December 1845, and hostilities commenced soon afterward.

When news of the war reached Stephen Watts Kearny, he was a middle-aged US Army colonel stationed at Fort Leavenworth. Kearny was ordered to immediately form a command called the "Army of the West," whose mission was to capture New Mexico and California from the Mexicans. To Kearny, the assignment was a challenge that would prove to be the high point of his career.

Kearny, an experienced veteran, was born in New Jersey in 1794. Barely old enough to see service in the War of 1812, he was, neverthe-less, commissioned a captain in 1813, and a few years later transferred to the "frontier." His association with mounted cavalry dated all the way back to the original formation of the US Regiment of Dragoons in 1833. At that time, Kearny was promoted to lieutenant colonel and second-in-command of this new mounted branch of the US Army. The dragoons were to be a crack outfit, and admittance to the new unit was limited to "healthy, respectable men, native citizens, not under twenty, nor over thirty-five years of age, whose size, figure and early pursuits may best qualify them for mounted soldiers."[1]

In 1836, when his commander, Colonel Henry Dodge, resigned from the army to become governor of Wisconsin Territory, Kearny himself assumed command of the Dragoons with the rank of colonel. From that point on, and for several years—although during 1836, a second regiment of dragoons was formed—Kearny served as the senior leader of the army's mounted troops. Kearny's reputation was also enhanced by the army's reliance on a book he had written. Entitled *Carbine Manual of Rules for the Exercise and Maneuvering of U.S. Dragoons*, the volume became the recognized authority on the use and care of American military shoulder arms.

General Stephen Watts Kearny. FROM *THE MILITARY OCCUPA- TION OF NEW MEXICO 1846–1851* / PUBLIC DOMAIN

Word of the war reached Colonel Kearny and his 1st Dragoons in mid-May at Fort Leavenworth. From Washington, DC, the secretary of war, William L. Marcy, sent Kearny a copy of the declaration. In a separate letter, the adjutant general of the US Army, Roger Jones, advised Kearny that a mounted force, most likely to be commanded by Kearny himself, would soon be assembled and sent to Santa Fe in order to protect US citizens and property. A letter signed by the secretary of war was also dispatched to the governor of Missouri, John C. Edwards, requesting him to immediately raise a regiment consisting of eight companies of mounted volunteers and two companies of volunteer artillery. The following day, Adjutant General Jones wrote to Colonel Kearny once again, this time confirming that he was to be the commander of the military force.[2]

Sixteen days later in Washington, President Polk and his Cabinet were seriously discussing the advisability of sending an army across the Santa Fe Trail to New Mexico this late in the season. Although it was only May, Polk was concerned whether American forces would have time to march to New Mexico, conquer the territory, and then march all the way to California before snow blocked the mountain passes. "In winter, all whom I had consulted agreed that it was impracticable to make the expedition,"[3] wrote President Polk in his diary. Thomas Hart Benton, the senior senator from Missouri, had different ideas. Benton, who only the previous month was hesitant about the speedy manner in which the United States had declared war on Mexico, was now one of the leading advocates for the rapid prosecution of the conflict. President Polk continued in his diary:

> *Col. Benton had brought me Frémont's [John Charles Frémont, who was Benton's son-in-law] map and book and given me much detailed information of the route and of the difficulties attending it, but advised the expedition this season provided it could move from Independence by the first of August.*[4]

Satisfied that Benton knew what he was talking about, Polk continued with his plans.

I finally submitted a distinct proposition to the Cabinet. Col. Kearny of the United States army was as I learned an experienced officer, and had been with a part of his regiment to the South Pass of the Rocky mountain, and made an extensive tour in that region last year. . . . The proposition which I submitted was that Col. Kearny should be ordered as soon as he took Santa Fe, if he thought it safe to do so and practicable for him to reach California before winter, to leave Santa Fe in charge of his Lieutenant–Colonel with a sufficient force to hold it, and proceed towards California with the balance of his command.[5]

Without debate, Polk's suggestions were approved by his Cabinet officers. Orders were written to Colonel Kearny, and he received them a few days after the President and his Cabinet conferred in Washington. In a letter dated June 3, 1846, from Secretary of War W. L. Marcy, Kearny was advised that:

It has been decided by the President to be of the greatest importance in the pending war with Mexico to take the earliest possession of Upper California. An expedition with that view is hereby ordered, and you are designated to command it.[6]

In the same letter, Kearny was informed that one thousand mounted Missouri troops would follow his command, and that if a larger element of volunteers was needed, he had the authority "to make a direct requisition for it upon the governor of Missouri."[7] While Marcy's directives left no doubt that President Polk fully expected Kearny to conquer New Mexico and California one way or the other, a peaceful occupation was preferred.

Should you conquer and take possession of New Mexico and Upper California . . . you will establish temporary civil governments therein. . . . In performing this duty it would be wise and prudent to continue in their employment all such of the existing officers as are known to be friendly to the United States, and will take the oath of allegiance to them. . . . You may assure the people of those provinces that it is the wish and design of the United States to provide for them a free government, with the least possible delay, similar to that which exists in our Territories. . . . In your whole conduct you will act in such a manner as best to conciliate the inhabitants and render them friendly to the United States.[8]

In the meantime, Governor Edwards of Missouri was busy raising the regiment of volunteers requested by President Polk. Companies of mounted volunteers were formed and filled across the state, and by June 5, they began arriving at Fort Leavenworth, where they were soon mustered into the regular service. While at the fort, the new recruits underwent rigorous training in dragoon tactics. John T. Hughes, a member of the 1st Regiment Missouri Mounted Volunteers, as the new unit was called, wrote about the training in his book *Doniphan's Expedition; Containing an Account of the Conquest of Mexico.*

For the space of twenty days, during which time portions of the volunteers remained at the fort, rigid drill twice per day, once before and after noon, was required to be performed by them,—in order to render their services the more efficient. These martial exercises, upon a small prairie adjacent to the fort, appropriately styled by the volunteers, "Campus Martis," consisting of the march by sections of four, the sabre exercises, the charge, the rally, and other cavalry tactics, doubtless proved subsequently to be of the most essential service.[9]

By June 18 all of the volunteer companies had arrived at Fort Leavenworth. As was the custom in volunteer forces, the men of the regiment elected their commander. The honor fell to Alexander W. Doniphan, who was a well-known lawyer, but who had volunteered in the 1st Missouri as a private. Now, with the rank of colonel, Doniphan was second-in-command, next to Colonel Kearny, of the entire Army of the West. By the latter part of June, Doniphan's regiment was ready to march with Kearny's dragoons to New Mexico.

With orders in hand Kearny rode out of Fort Leavenworth in late June of 1846, accompanied by a mixed army of 1,658 men. Consisting of 300

troopers of his own 1st Dragoons; 856 mounted riflemen of the 1st Regiment Missouri Mounted Volunteers, under the command of Colonel
Doniphan; 250 artillerymen from St. Louis; 145 infantrymen from Missouri; and 107 Laclede Rangers from St. Louis, the Army of the West
soon picked up the Santa Fe Trail and pointed itself toward Bent's Fort,
some 537 miles to the west.

The logistics of the first leg of Kearny's mission—to reach Bent's
Fort—were mind-boggling. With him were 3,658 mules, 14,904 cattle,
459 extra horses, and 1,556 wagons. His artillery command consisted
of twelve six-pounder cannons and four twelve-pounder howitzers. The
sheer magnitude of managing men and materiel of such proportions
across hundreds of miles of hot, dry prairie was staggering. But the old
veteran Kearny, with the same resourcefulness and determination that he
had used years earlier to make his dragoons such a success, prevailed, and
the trip to Bent's Fort proved to be relatively uneventful.

For most of the men, the first part of the journey across the plains
was rather enjoyable. John T. Hughes described some of the more pleasant moments in his book:

> We crossed the river [the Kansas] without loss or accident, and
> encamped for the night on the west bank among friendly Shawnees.
> Some of the Shawnees have large farms, and as fine fields of corn as
> are to be met with in the States. They also have plenty of poultry,
> domestic animals, fine gardens, and many of the luxuries of civilized
> life. Here we obtained milk and butter; also peas, beans, potatoes,
> and other vegetables. The country between Fort Leavenworth and
> the Kansas is very fine; the soil is exceedingly fertile,—vegetation is
> exuberant; and in many places the timber is tall and stately.[10]

As the miles that separated the army from Fort Leavenworth length-
ened, however, conditions along the Trail become more severe. On the
morning of July 12 the temperature was 95 degrees, and mirages fooled
the mounted soldiers into seeing water that was not really there. Provisions were running low. Kearny's regimental adjutant, Lieutenant Abraham Robinson Johnston, declared:

[F]rom the sand hills on the south side of the river there came blasts of hot air almost stifling. . . . The small tributaries of the Arkansas begin to show small patches of trees upon them. The willows and cottonwood are springing up in the bottoms, indicating the progress of the forest over the prairie.[11]

Johnston could not have known that he was predicting the future of the region when he remarked in his journal, "Keep fire away from it [the prairie] and in one hundred years it would be one of the richest portions of the continent."[12]

Finally, however, the Arkansas River was sighted, and "Horse and man ran involuntarily into the river, and simultaneously slaked their burning thirst."[13] Herds of buffalo appeared on the endless prairies, and many were killed, cooked, and heartily devoured by the hungry soldiers.

In late July, lead elements of the Army of the West approached Bent's Fort. A difficult first part of the journey was now over. As the soldiers drew nearer to the fort, the mountain man Thomas "Broken Hand" Fitzpatrick, who had guided Colonel Kearny to the Rocky Mountains and back the previous year, rode up with a message for the colonel. Fitzpatrick's message related that New Mexico's governor, Manuel Armijo, was presently preparing all parts of New Mexico for the imminent invasion by the American army, and that Kearny's "movements would be vigorously opposed."[14]

Governor Armijo was not very popular with Colonel Kearny. Although the two men had never met, Kearny no doubt remembered Armijo's role in the 1841 Texan–Santa Fe Expedition, and how he had forcibly marched, under armed guard, scores of Texans to Mexico City for detention. And, he still had memories of the 1843 attack of a Texas soldier of fortune, Jacob Snively, upon an advance party of Armijo's army that was traveling up the Santa Fe Trail in today's Kansas, on its way to protect a Mexican trading caravan. Snively's men killed seventeen Mexicans and captured eighty-two others. Men of Kearny's own 1st Dragoons were sent out, under the command of Captain Philip St. George Cooke, to intercept and arrest Snively's men after the incident caused a national uproar.

Colonel Kearny took Armijo's threats into consideration as he prepared to plot his next move—the actual occupation of New Mexico—in as painless and bloodless a manner as possible.

Although Bent's Fort, sprawled alongside the Santa Fe Trail, was never designed to accommodate as large a number of men as arrived there in late July, nevertheless, the owners and managers scurried about to ensure that the soldiers were as comfortable as possible. For the short time that members of the Army of the West spent at the fort, most of them bivouacked on the flat lands nine miles downstream.

Santa Fe, the target of the first phase of Colonel Kearny's operations, was only about a two-week journey on the Trail from Bent's Fort. So, while the men and animals of his mixed command rested for the upcoming march, Kearny availed himself of the opportunity to compose a directive which he intended to distribute to the population along the way to Santa Fe. Dated July 31, 1846, the proclamation read:

> *The undersigned enters New Mexico with a large military force, for the purpose of seeking union with and ameliorating the conditions of its inhabitants. This he does under instructions from his government, and with the assurance that he will be amply sustained in the accomplishment of this object. It is enjoined on the citizens of New Mexico to remain quietly at their homes, and to pursue their peaceful avocations. So long as they continue in such pursuits, they will not be interfered with by the American army, but will be respected and protected in their rights, both civil and religious.*
>
> *All who take up arms or encourage resistance against the government of the United States will be regarded as enemies, and will be treated accordingly.*[15]

On August 2, the Army of the West broke camp at Bent's Fort and began its southwestward march along the Santa Fe Trail toward Raton Pass. Once on the other side of the Arkansas River, Kearny and his men found themselves on that parcel of land claimed by both Texas and Mexico. For all practical purposes, from this point on, the army was invading enemy territory. Four days later found elements of the army approaching Raton Pass. First Lieutenant William H. Emory, a topographical engineer with Colonel Kearny's command, recorded the events in his journal:

> *[W]e commenced the ascent of the Raton, and, after marching 17 miles, halted, with the infantry and general staff, within a half mile of the summit of the pass. Strong parties were sent forward to repair the road, which winds through a picturesque valley, with the Raton towering to the left. . . . The view from our camp is inexpressibly beautiful and reminds persons of the landscape of Palestine. . . . The road is well-located. The general appearance is something like the pass at the summit of the Boston and Albany railroad, but the scenery bolder, and less adorned with vegetation.*[16]

The following day, the crossing was made, and Lieutenant Emory's barometer showed the height of Raton Pass to be 7,500 feet above sea level.

Another topographical engineer, Second Lieutenant J. W. Abert, had started out with Colonel Kearny's command, but due to sickness he had to be left behind at Bent's Fort. When he continued his journey to Santa Fe some weeks after Kearny had already departed, Abert himself crossed Raton Pass. In his diary he confirmed the difficulty that wagons had in negotiating the treacherous gap in the mountains:

> *[W]e commenced the passage of one of the most rocky roads I ever saw; no one who has crossed the Raton can ever forget it. A dense growth of pitch pine interferes with the guidance of the teams; in many places the axletrees were frayed against the huge fragments of rock that jutted up between the wheels as we passed; pieces of broken wagons lined the road, and at the foot of the hill we saw many axletrees, wagon tongues, sand-boards, and ox yokes, that had been broken and cast aside.*[17]

On the day after the Army of the West crossed Raton Pass, Governor Armijo issued a proclamation of this own. Written on August 8, at Santa Fe, the announcement read:

Fellow Countrymen:—At last the moment has arrived when our country requires of her children a decision without limit, a sacrifice without reserve, under circumstances which claim all for our salvation.

Questions with the United States of America which have been treated with dignity and decorum by the supreme magistrate of the Republic, remain undetermined as claimed as unquestionable rights of Mexico over the usurped Territory of Texas, and on account of this it has been impossible to assume diplomatic relations with the government of North America, whose minister extraordinary has not been received; but the forces of that government are advancing in this department; they have crossed the northern frontier and at present are near. . . .

Hear, then, fellow citizens and countrymen, the signal of alarm which must prepare us for battle. . . .

Today . . . sacred independence, the fruit of so many and costly sacrifices, is threatened, for if we are not capable of maintaining the integrity of our territory, it will all soon be the prey of the avarice and enterprise of our neighbors from the north, and nothing will remain but a sad recollection of our political existence. . . .

Fellow citizens and countrymen, united with the regular army, you will strengthen the sentiments of loyalty among your defenders. Now to the call! Let us be comrades in arms and, with honest union, we shall lead to victory. . . .

Rest assured that your governor is willing and ready to sacrifice his life and all his interests in the defense of his country. This you will see demonstrated by your chief, fellow-countryman and friend.[18]

Once on the other side of Raton Pass, Kearny's men found that travel was much easier, since the terrain soon became relatively flat. The Army of the West was now eight days out of Bent's Fort, and Kearny knew that his command was traveling deep into enemy territory. Along the trail, a party of Mexicans, whose mission was to reconnoiter the American forces, was captured. In a humorous aside from the serious business of war, the Mexicans must have made quite a negative impression on Kearny's men. In the words of Emory, "They were mounted on diminutive asses, and

The Army of the West. FROM *THE MILITARY OCCUPATION OF NEW MEXICO 1846–1851* / PUBLIC DOMAIN

presented a ludicrous contrast by side of the big men and horses of the first dragoons." Thomas Fitzpatrick, the famed mountain man who was serving Kearny as a scout, "became almost convulsed whenever he turned his well practised [*sic*] eye in their direction."[19]

In a more sober vein, however, reports of continuing unrest gradually made their way to the army. Emory wrote on August 10:

> *Mr. Towle, an American citizen, came to headquarters . . . and reported himself just escaped from Taos. He brought the intelligence that, yesterday, the proclamation of Governor Armijo reached there, calling the citizens to arms, and placing the whole country under martial law; that Armijo has assembled all the Pueblo Indians, numbering about 2,000, and all the citizens capable of bearing arms; that 300 Mexican dragoons arrived at Santa Fe the day Armijo's proclamation was issued, and that 1,200 more were hourly expected; that the Mexicans to a man were anxious for a fight, but that half the Pueblo Indians were indifferent on the subject, but would be made to fight.*[20]

On the following day, Lieutenant Emory continued in his journal:

Matters are now becoming very interesting. Six or eight Mexicans were captured last night, and on their persons was found the proclamation of the Prefect of Taos, based upon that of Armijo, calling the citizens to arms, to "repel the Americans, who were coming to invade their soil and destroy their property and liberties"; ordering an enrolment [sic] of all citizens over 15 and under 50.[21]

Two days later an American named Spry entered Kearny's camp with additional reports of Mexican unrest. Spry had escaped from detention in Santa Fe the night before. He had intelligence that a Mexican army, led by Governor Armijo, was gathering at Apache Canyon a few miles east of Santa Fe, and that the force intended to make a stand against the American army there. Undaunted, Kearny and his tired men continued their march toward Santa Fe. On August 14 extra precautions were taken among the men, and an order of march was devised so that a battle formation could be formed immediately. Later in the day, a letter from Armijo was delivered to Kearny. Emory's report reveals that the letter, literally translated, stated:

You have notified me that you intend to take possession of the country I govern. The people of the country have risen en masse in my defence. If you take the country, it will be because you prove the strongest in battle.[22]

On the evening of August 14, the men of the Army of the West made camp on the outskirts of the small village of Vegas, today's town of Las Vegas, New Mexico, located about sixty miles from Santa Fe. Around midnight, information was received by Colonel Kearny that six hundred Mexicans, fully prepared for battle, had assembled at a pass located two miles from the American encampment. At eight o'clock on the morning of August 15, Kearny, who had just received word of his promotion to brigadier general, rode into the village. Amid the stares of scores of curious farmers and townspeople, General Kearny climbed to the roof of a low building on the Plaza and announced the American occupation of New Mexico.[23]

General Kearny was surprised when none of the Vegas villagers offered resistance. Several of the leading citizens took the oath of allegiance to the United States, and in a matter of hours, the Army of the West departed for its rendezvous with the six hundred Mexican soldiers who supposedly still awaited them in the pass outside the village. However, the information proved to be false, and no Mexican army was to be seen. The men of the 1st Dragoons, anxious for a fight, ended the day disappointed.

The village of San Miguel was reached the next day, and after General Kearny assembled the officials and leading citizens, he made a speech similar to the one he had given at Vegas. Reports of the massive buildup of the enemy at Apache Canyon became more frequent now, and in the midafternoon, a messenger rode up to General Kearny and exclaimed, "They are in the Cañon, my brave; pluck up your courage and push them out."[24]

On the following day, a rumor reached the American camp that the two thousand Mexican soldiers under Governor Armijo, supposedly gathered at Apache Canyon, had fled. Indeed, they had, and for reasons that only General Kearny and a few of his trusted staff were aware.

On August 1, from Bent's Fort, General Kearny had dispatched James Wiley Magoffin, accompanied by Captain Philip St. George Cooke, to Santa Fe to meet with Governor Armijo and to attempt to persuade him to allow the Army of the West to enter the city and to occupy New Mexico unopposed. Magoffin had been summoned to Washington, DC, the previous June and had met with Senator Thomas Hart Benton and President Polk to discuss the possibility of his participation in an effort to keep Kearny's campaign as uneventful as possible. Polk was impressed with Magoffin and wrote in his diary that "he is a very intelligent man and gave me much valuable information."[25] Benton already was acquainted with Magoffin, as he was one of Missouri's foremost Santa Fe traders. Since Magoffin knew the New Mexican people and the countryside intimately, Benton felt that his presence with the advancing

American army "could be of infinite service to the invading force."[26] Magoffin had agreed to assist Kearny and left Washington immediately. It was not until he reached Bent's Fort on July 26 that he caught up with the Army of the West, as well as with his own brother, Samuel, and sister-in-law, Susan. Samuel and Susan had departed Independence, Missouri, on June 11, 1846, as part of a large trading caravan on its way to Santa Fe. When the Magoffin wagons reached Bent's Fort, its members had awaited the arrival of Colonel Kearny and his men.

Magoffin and Cooke arrived in Santa Fe on August 12, carrying the letter for Armijo written by Kearny on August 1. When the governor read the communication, he was surprised to learn that, according to Kearny, the United States was only interested in the part of New Mexico that lay east of the Rio Grande. Kearny pleaded with Armijo to submit to the American army, emphasizing that resistance would be futile, and that the defeat which Armijo's forces were certain to undergo would only alienate him with the Mexican government and the population at large.

The exact details of the meeting have never been revealed, and it is impossible to know what promises, if any, Armijo made regarding the defense of Santa Fe. His reply of August 12 to Kearny's letter does not mention the meeting with the American emissaries, nor does it reference a potential retreat of his armed forces, nor a decision to lessen the New Mexican defenses. It does declare, however, that Armijo believed his troops to be sufficient in strength and arms to resist the American threat. In retrospect, it appears that by the time Santa Fe was being approached by the Army of the West, Armijo was creating a sham to protect himself from what he knew would be unrelenting criticism—not only from the central government in Mexico City, but from an irate constituency as well—if they ever discovered that he had lessened his ardor to protect New Mexico without making an effort to fight.

Magoffin later persuaded Governor Armijo's second-in-command, Colonel Diego Archuleta, to offer no resistance to the American take-over—when he pointed out that all of the territory west of the Rio Grande might be his for the taking—since the United States lacked interest in that part of New Mexico. Of course, the falsehood of that statement would soon become apparent to Archuleta when he later read

General Kearny's proclamation of August 22, in which it became clear that the United States intended to occupy both banks of the Rio Grande.

In any event, for the time being, the American agent Magoffin had supposedly obtained acquiescence to a peaceful takeover of Santa Fe and the rest of New Mexico by American military forces. Therefore, when Apache Canyon was approached by the Army of the West on August 18, Kearny found that Armijo had, indeed, lived up to his promise and called off the defense of the canyon.[27]

Unaware of the real reason for the retreat of Armijo's army, Lieutenant Emory, the senior topographical engineer with Kearny, later wrote the following in his report:

Reliable information, from several sources, had reached camp yesterday and the day before, that dissensions had arisen in Armijo's camp, which had dispersed his army, and that he had fled to the south, carrying all his artillery and 100 dragoons with him. Not a hostile rifle or arrow was now between the army and Santa Fe, the capital of New Mexico, and the general determined to make the march in one day, and raise the United States flag over the palace before sundown. New horses and mules were ordered for the artillery, and everything was braced up for a forced march. The distance was not great, but the road bad, and the horses on their last legs.[28]

Actually, Kearny's command was only twenty-nine miles from Santa Fe, and the arduous drive toward the town was begun. When the men had marched about fourteen miles they came upon the defile that Governor Armijo had recently deserted. According to Emory,

It is a gateway which, in the hands of a skillful engineer and one hundred resolute men, would have been perfectly impregnable. Had the position been defended with any resolution, the general [Kearny] would have been obliged to turn it by a road which branches to the south, six miles from Pecos, by the way of Galisteo.

Armijo's arrangements for defence were very stupid. His abattis [sic] was placed behind the gorge some 100 yards, by which he

evidently intended that the gorge should be passed before his fire was opened. This done, and his batteries would have been carried without difficulty.[29]

When they reached Armijo's deserted position in the canyon, the soldiers of General Kearny's command were jubilant. Unaware of the secret negotiations in Santa Fe by Magoffin a few evenings before, the proud soldiers gloried in their military prowess, confident that the Mexican army had fled out of fear.

At around noon on August 18, General Kearny was approached by two Mexicans, one of them the acting secretary of state. The men carried a letter from the lieutenant governor—now the acting governor in Armijo's absence—assuring Kearny that he would encounter no resistance, and extending to him any hospitalities that the town could afford. Advance elements of the American army arrived in Santa Fe at around three o'clock in the afternoon, and the rear guard pulled into town three hours later. Lieutenant Governor Juan Bautista Vigil y Alarid and a score of local dignitaries met Kearny and his staff and served them refreshments consisting of wine and brandy.

As the Americans enjoyed the hospitality of the Mexican officials at the ancient Palace of the Governors, they watched at sunset as the Mexican flag was lowered and the Stars and Stripes was run up the flagstaff. From the high ground behind the Palace, thirteen cannons saluted the occasion. Afterward, Kearny's staff was invited to dinner, which, according to Emory,

was served very much after the manner of a French dinner, one dish succeeding another in endless variety. A bottle of good wine from the Passo de Norte, and a loaf of bread was placed at each plate. We had been since five in the morning without eating, and inexhaustible as were the dishes was our appetite.[30]

The Santa Fe that the Army of the West occupied that hot August day in 1846 was a small Mexican town that had been founded in the opening years of the seventeenth century. At the time of its establishment, it was the northernmost town in New Spain. Now, in the mid-1800s, the village numbered between two thousand and three thousand souls, mostly merchants, the clergy, and farmers. Lieutenant Emory recorded in his notes that "the inhabitants are, it is said, the poorest people of any town in the province." Continuing his description of the village and its people, Emory added:

The houses are of mud bricks, in the Spanish style, generally of one story, and built on a square. The interior of the square is an open court, and the principal rooms open into it. They are forbidding in appearance from the outside, but nothing can exceed the comfort and convenience of the interior. The thick walls make them cool in summer and warm in the winter.

The better class of people are provided with excellent beds, but the lower class sleep on untanned skins. The women here, as in many other parts of the world, appear to be much before the men in refinement, and knowledge of the useful arts. The higher class dress like the American women, except, instead of the bonnet, they wear a scarf over the head. This they wear, asleep or awake, in the house or abroad.

The dress of the lower class of women is a simple petticoat with arms and shoulders bare, except what may chance to be covered by the reboso [sic] [a woman's scarf].

The men who have means to do so, dress after our fashion; but by far the greater number, when they dress at all, wear leather breeches, tight around the hips and open from the knee down; shirt and blanket take the place of coat and vest.[31]

When Lieutenant Abert arrived in Santa Fe in September, he recorded a vivid description of the Plaza, where most of the town's business and trade were pursued. Abert wrote:

On the north side is the palace, occupying the whole side of the square. On the remaining sides one finds the stores of the merchants and traders, and in the centre of the square a tall flag staff has been erected, from which the banner of freedom now waves. There all the country people congregate to sell their marketing, and one constantly sees objects to amuse. Trains of "burros" are continually entering the city, laden with kegs of Taos whiskey or immense packs of fodder, melons, wood, or grapes. Our own soldiers, too, are constantly passing and repassing, or mingling with the motley groups of Mexicans and Pueblo Indians.[32]

John T. Hughes, the volunteer with Doniphan's regiment, reported that, small as Santa Fe was, the town contained six Catholic churches. But, there were "no public schools, the business of education being entrusted to ecclesiastics." Hughes wrote that "the streets are crooked and narrow," adding "The whole presents very much the appearance of an extensive brickyard."[33]

The day after the American army arrived in Santa Fe, General Kearny assembled a great many of the town's residents in the Plaza and addressed them in much the same fashion as he had the people of San Miguel and Las Vegas. When he completed his speech, the former lieutenant governor, Juan Bautista Vigil y Alarid, took the platform and responded:

The inhabitants of this Department humbly and honorably present their loyalty and allegiance to the government of North America. No one in this world can successfully resist the power of him who is stronger.

Continuing, Vigil added:

Do not find it strange if there has been no manifestation of joy and enthusiasm in seeing this city occupied by your military forces. To us the power of the Mexican Republic is dead. No matter what her condition, she was our mother. What child will not shed abundant tears at the tomb of his parents? . . . To-day we belong to a great and powerful nation. Its flag, with its stars and stripes, covers the horizon of New Mexico, and its brilliant light shall grow like good seed well cultivated. We are cognizant of your kindness, of your courtesy and that of your accommodating officers and of the strict discipline of your troops; we know that we belong to the Republic that owes its origin to the immortal Washington, whom all civilized nations admire and respect. . . . In the name, then, of the entire Department, I swear obedience to the Northern Republic and I tender my respect to its laws and authority.[34]

On the next day, August 20, several leaders of the nearby pueblos came to meet with Kearny and to "express their great satisfaction at our arrival."[35] The chiefs gave Kearny their promises of allegiance to the United States, and a gleeful Lieutenant Emory wrote, "They and the numerous half-breeds are our fast friends now and forever."[36] More delegations of residents visited with Kearny and his staff during the remainder of the week, leaving the Americans with a feeling of security and a job well done.

The American occupation of New Mexico was nearly complete. On August 22 General Kearny issued a tersely worded proclamation to the people of Santa Fe in which no doubt was left of his expectations.[37] Kearny was obviously now pleased with himself and his Army of the West. He had fulfilled the first part of his orders to the letter, and all the better without bloodshed. On the same day that Kearny issued his proclamation, he also sent a letter to General Jonathan E. Wool, the American commander at Chihuahua. In it he proudly reiterated, "I have to inform you, that on the 18th instant, without firing a gun or spilling a drop of blood, I took possession of this city, the capital of the department of New Mexico."[38] Kearny's destiny now lay in far-off California, and his involvement with the Santa Fe Trail was over.

Chapter Eleven

The Santa Fe Trail during the 1850s and 1860s

By the time the middle of the nineteenth century arrived, the Santa Fe Trail had been a highway of American commerce for nearly three decades. According to Josiah Gregg's figures in his book, *Commerce of the Prairies*, the 1840s had been particularly busy years. The last entry provided by Gregg, for 1843, showed that almost half a million dollars' worth of goods were sent down the Trail that year aboard 230 wagons and accompanied by 350 men.

The 1850s saw a continuation of the trend. More and more traffic rolled along the Trail with each passing year. By 1855 merchandise valued at $5 million was being hauled from Missouri to Santa Fe and southward into Mexico. By 1860 more than nine thousand men and in excess of six thousand mules, three thousand wagons, and nearly twenty-eight thousand oxen were required to keep up with the exchange of goods between New Mexico and the markets back East.

In the meantime, the US Army found it desirable to build a fort in New Mexico to house its 1,300 soldiers in the territory and to protect the region's citizens from Indians. Heretofore, army garrisons had been distributed among the many villages scattered across the countryside, and control and discipline of the soldiers were difficult to maintain. The secretary of war felt that "removing the troops out of the towns . . . and stationing them more toward the frontier, nearer the Indians" would result in "both economy and efficiency of the service."[1]

The new fort was located near the southern junction of the Cimarron Cutoff branch of the Santa Fe Trail and the Mountain Branch, that part which ran past Bent's Fort and eked its way through Raton Pass on the New Mexican border with Colorado. The post was begun in August 1851, and upon its completion, it was named Fort Union.

Unfortunately for those stationed at Fort Union, the experience was less than desirable. One officer's wife, several years after her residence there, wrote, "Many ladies dislike Fort Union. It has always been noted for severe duststorms [*sic*]."[2] Additionally, most of the structures making up the fort had been built by the soldiers themselves, and their unskilled hands did little to provide a durable, long-lasting compound. Only five years after completion, an officer remarked that

> [u]nseasoned, unhewn, and unbarked pine logs, placed upright in some and horizontally in other houses, have been used in the erection of the buildings, and as a necessary consequence are rapidly decaying. In many of the logs of the house I occupy, an ordinary sized nail will not hold, to such an extent has the timber decayed. . . . One set of the so-called barracks have lately been torn down to prevent any untoward accidents that are liable at any moment to happen from the falling of the building.[3]

As the old structures within the fort continued to deteriorate, and as the impending Civil War grew closer, a new fort was begun in 1861, located east of the old one. The new post was built in the shape of a star, but it afforded no better living conditions than the first Fort Union. By the time it was completed the following year, the Confederate Army had already retreated from New Mexico, and the need for the new star fort had greatly lessened.

The Confederate invasion of New Mexico that had made the construction of the star fort necessary in the first place was short-lived. The Confederate Territory of Arizona, which included New Mexico, had been organized in August 1861, and by the end of the year, about twenty-five hundred soldiers were gathered at Fort Bliss, near El Paso.

General Henry H. Sibley—the nephew of George Sibley, who had surveyed the Santa Fe Trail back in 1825—commanded the Confederate forces, and he planned to move out of Fort Bliss and to quickly occupy Albuquerque, Santa Fe, and Fort Union. Sibley's ultimate goal was to reach Denver, where he intended to declare the entire Southwest for the Confederacy. The Union Army, under the command of Colonel E. R. S. Canby, was gathered at Fort Craig, located about halfway between El Paso and Albuquerque. The opposing armies clashed there in February 1862, as Sibley's men attempted to skirt around the fort on their way to Albuquerque.

The Confederates won the day and continued their push northward. Soon, the Union garrisons at both Albuquerque and Santa Fe retreated to the safety of Fort Union. In the meantime, a Colorado volunteer army made its way through a late winter's blizzard to help protect the post. On March 11 the volunteers arrived at the fort, totally exhausted from their frantic march down the Santa Fe Trail from Colorado.

In late March, General Sibley's Southern army met with the soldiers from Fort Union and the Colorado volunteers at Glorieta Pass on the Trail, southeast of Santa Fe. For a while during the fierce conflict, the Confederates appeared to have won the battle. However, in the meantime, Union soldiers located and destroyed Sibley's supply wagons, leaving the Confederates with no ammunition, food, or clothing.

Sibley's troops retreated all the way back to Fort Bliss, and the Confederate Territory of Arizona ceased to exist. The Battle of Glorieta Pass was one of the most decisive conflicts fought west of the Mississippi River during the entire Civil War. As a result of this battle, the South lost its one chance to make New Mexico and Arizona part of the Confederacy, and the region remained under the influence of the Union Army throughout the remainder of the conflict.

With New Mexico secured for the Union, plans were made to build Fort Union once more. For six years, from 1863 until 1869, the new Fort Union was under construction. Located beside the ill-fated star fort, the new installation became a combination garrison for soldiers, a quartermaster's depot for supplies, and an ordnance (or weapons) depot. It was the largest US Army post in New Mexico, and one of the most important installations in the entire West.

Fort Union served its role as protector of the Santa Fe Trail until 1891, more than a decade after its effectiveness had been severely curtailed due to the arrival of the railroad. A local newspaper article dated February 18 ruefully revealed that

> *[t]he last days have told a terrible tale at Fort Union. Four days ago everything was in running order; now everything is upside down and inside out. . . . The soldiers are busy packing government and private property.*[4]

Of course, the business of freighting had continued over the Santa Fe Trail during all of these precarious war years. In fact, the existence and sheer size of Fort Union demanded a vast amount of supplies to be shipped over the Trail during the mid- and late 1860s. As one of the army's most remote—yet most important—posts west of the Mississippi River, it was urgent that it be well supplied at all times, and the Santa Fe Trail still served as a viable link in the communications network with operations back East.

Two other important army posts were built along the Trail during this period of time. Fort Larned, Kansas, located on the Pawnee Fork of the Arkansas River, was established in 1859. For many years, the post was the most significant army installation on the eastern part of the Trail. Fort Larned, in addition to its role as protector of the Trail, served as the agency for several tribes of southern Great Plains Indians, including the Cheyenne, Arapaho, Kiowa, and Comanche tribes.

Later, Fort Larned provided protection for the crews of men who marched relentlessly across the prairie, surveying rights-of-way for the rail lines, as well as for those who were actually involved in the construction of the railroad. By 1878, however, Fort Larned was no longer an important element of the Santa Fe Trail, and the post was abandoned by the army.

Fort Dodge was built in the western section of Kansas in 1864. It was situated near the northern junction of the Cimarron Cutoff and the Mountain Branch of the Trail. Its strategic location made it an important post for the army during the days of Indian warfare on the southern Great Plains. It was abandoned in 1882 after it had served its purpose as a mustering point for escort parties organized to protect wagon trains along the Trail during the 1860s and 1870s. Over the years, the army built other posts along the Santa Fe Trail, but Forts Union, Larned, and Dodge were probably the most important ones.

One of the most elaborate and difficult efforts to make improvements upon the Santa Fe Trail was begun in 1866 by a former mountain man and Trail freighter named Richens Lacy Wootton, known to his friends as "Uncle Dick." Wootton was a Virginian by birth, but had moved west at an early age. He counted as his friends such contemporaries as the

"Uncle Dick" Wootton. FROM *"UNCLE DICK" WOOTTON* / PUBLIC DOMAIN

Bent brothers, Kit Carson, Jim Bridger, and other men famous in Western history.

In Wootton's autobiography, *"Uncle Dick" Wootton*, published in 1890, Uncle Dick explained what he wanted to do to improve the trail and why he wanted to do it.

> *I had long had in mind the building of a stage road through the "Raton Pass," and when I made up my mind to quit farming . . . I thought it a good time to put through my road project. I had been over the mountains so often . . . that I knew almost every available pass in Colorado and New Mexico. . . . I knew that the Raton Pass was a natural highway, connecting settlements already in existence, and destined to be a thoroughfare for other settlements. . . . How to get through the pass, was the problem. . . . A trail led through the canyon it is true, but that was almost impassable for anything but saddle horses and pack animals at any time, and entirely impassable for wagon trains or stages in the winter time. . . . What I proposed to do was to go into this winding, rock-ribbed mountain pass, and hew out a road, which barring grades, should be as good as the average turnpike.[5]*

Wootton applied to both the Colorado and New Mexico governments for charters to build his road. When it was all approved, he began his gigantic effort. He later wrote:

> *I had untaken no light task, I can assure you. There were hillsides to cut down, rocks to blast and remove, and bridges to build by the score. I built the road, however, and made it a good one too. . . . My twenty-seven miles of turnpike constituted a portion of an international thoroughfare.[6]*

Uncle Dick built his home on the Colorado side of Raton Pass, and when he was through with his construction project, the turnpike he had built greatly enhanced travel for wagons on the Mountain Branch of the Santa Fe Trail. Wootton had once accompanied a wagon train over Raton Pass in 1858, and it had taken him almost a month to travel fifty miles, so steep and treacherous was the pathway. With the new improvements, wagons could now make the same passage in a few days.

In order to pay for his road, Uncle Dick charged a toll for all passengers who used it. The concept immediately ran into trouble when Wootton discovered that he "had to deal with a great many people who seemed to think that they should be as free to travel over my well graded and bridged roadway, as they were to follow an ordinary cow path."[7]

Wootton divided his potential customers into five categories: the stage company and its employees, the freighters, the military, the Mexicans, and the Indians. He wisely decided not to charge the Indians, and he related well with the stage people, the army, and the freighters. However, he lamented:

> *My Mexican patrons were the hardest to get along with. Paying for the privilege of traveling over any road was something they were totally unused to, and they did not take to it kindly. They were pleased with my road and liked to travel over it until they reached the toll gate.*[8]

But Wootton persisted, sometimes resolving his toll-gate problems "through diplomacy, and sometimes . . . with a club."[9] Business was good, reaping Wootton several thousands of dollars in revenue during the twelve-year period, from 1866 until 1878, that he operated the toll road.

Eventually, though, even Uncle Dick's modern turnpike was outdated. As the railroad extended its terminus farther and farther west with each succeeding year, the Santa Fe Trail's importance to shipping diminished. Before long, the Trail would be forgotten in the wake of the speed and economy of the railroad.

CHAPTER TWELVE

The Railroad and the End
of the Santa Fe Trail

RAILROADS HAD THEIR BEGINNINGS IN AMERICA IN THE EARLY 1830S, when horses pulled a modified stagecoach along a pair of iron rails laid across the ground. Progress in this exciting new mode of travel was rapid, however, and by the time the 1850s arrived, trains consisting of many cars and pulled by locomotives that ran on steam were traveling among the major cities of the East. By 1854 the railroad had reached the Mississippi River, and two years later had crossed to the western side. In 1869 the continent was finally bridged when two lines, one from the East and one from the West, linked up in Utah to form the nation's first transcontinental railroad.

Two different rail lines vied for the honor of reaching New Mexico first. The Atchison, Topeka and Santa Fe (AT&SF) Railway had arrived at Pueblo, Colorado, in 1876. Its next expansion was a section through the treacherous mountains of the Raton Pass area. In the meantime, the Denver & Rio Grande line had laid its tracks as far south as Moro, Colorado, and it also stood ready to survey a route through Raton.

Uncle Dick Wootton favored the AT&SF line. In February 1878, when engineers from the railroad arrived in southern Colorado to begin their survey through the mountains, Wootton and some of the local townspeople from nearby Trinidad assisted them so they could beat the Denver & Rio Grande surveyors, who had reached the area the same day.

The AT&SF surveyors won the contest, and consequently, the "Santa Fe" railroad, as it was now being called, became the dominant line to serve northern New Mexico. To honor Wootton for his valuable assistance in getting the railroad completed, grateful AT&SF officials named the first locomotive used on the run through Raton Pass the "Uncle Dick." Wootton, his wife, and his invalid daughter also received lifetime pensions, and the entire Wootton family was awarded lifetime passes on the train.

In early July 1879, the Santa Fe line reached Las Vegas, New Mexico, a few miles southwest of Fort Union. The event signaled the end of an era. No longer would the Santa Fe Trail be needed to resupply the fort. In fact, the post itself lost its importance, since the railroad allowed men and materiel to be shuttled across the southern Great Plains with breakneck speed. Although Fort Union continued as an active army post for another decade, the Santa Fe Trail died then and there, with the lonesome whistle of the locomotive named "Uncle Dick" ringing in its ears.

During the summer of 1879, work on the Santa Fe railroad resumed, and tracks were laid through Glorieta Pass and then across the flatlands, to Lamy. Ironically, the main line was never laid all the way to its namesake,

The AT&SF Railway's climb to Raton Pass. COURTESY OF DENVER PUBLIC LIBRARY

Santa Fe. Instead, a short spur connected the capital city and Lamy, a few miles away. Consequently, the main rail line entered Albuquerque following a more-direct route.

For close to sixty years the Santa Fe Trail ruled supreme as the primary means of transportation of people, animals, and freight from the Missouri settlements to the frontiers of New Mexico. With the arrival of the railroad, that supremacy was gone. The Trail was soon forgotten, except to those thousands of Americans who had traveled along its scarred furrows to see the fabled lands of New Mexico and to trade with its inhabitants.

Prairie grass eventually grew over the myriad tracks etched by the countless numbers of wagons that had labored over the Trail. Season after season of dry heat and fierce rainstorm beat upon the Trail's worn path until, in a few years, nothing was left of the old thoroughfare except occasional ruts in the tall grass. Some of these ruts are still visible today, and as long as they remain, there will always be a Santa Fe Trail to remind present and future generations of the hardships, dedication, and foresight possessed by those westward-facing individuals who made a highway out of a wilderness path.

CHAPTER THIRTEEN

The Santa Fe Trail Today

FREIGHT WAGONS CEASED TO ROLL ACROSS THE SANTA FE TRAIL NEARLY 150 years ago. Displaced first by the railroad, then by a modern highway system, remnants of the old Trail, nevertheless, can still be seen in places along the way. And, fortunately for today's generation, there are many important places associated with the Santa Fe Trail during its heyday that are still in existence today.

On May 8, 1987, President Ronald Reagan signed a bill that established the Santa Fe National Historic Trail, making the old highway part of the National Trails System. The National Trails System Act was passed in 1968 in order "to provide for the outdoor recreation needs of an expanding population" and "to promote the preservation of, public access to, travel within, and enjoyment and appreciation of the open-air, outdoor areas and historic resources of our nation."

Today's Santa Fe National Historic Trail generally follows the original Santa Fe Trail. From Old Franklin, Missouri, it winds across that state, as well as across Kansas, Oklahoma, Colorado, and New Mexico, until it ends up in Santa Fe. One can drive an automobile along several sections of the Trail, since modern roadways have in some instances followed the original route. However, most of the Trail cuts cross-country, over farms and ranches that were part of the vast open prairie when the original Trail was being traveled.

Listed below are some of the more-important sites that are associated with the history of the Santa Fe Trail. A visit to these sites gives one the feeling of what it was like to have been a traveler along the Trail in bygone days.

Missouri Sites

1. **Site of Franklin**. Although the original town of Franklin was washed away by the Missouri River in 1828, the site itself is important since it was the jumping-off place for William Becknell's first Santa Fe trip in 1821.

2. **Fort Osage**. Fort Osage was not situated on the Santa Fe Trail, but the 1825 government survey of the Trail started there. Today, Fort Osage has been reconstructed and provides an interesting insight into life as it existed in what, at one time, was the country's western-most army facility and most profitable fur factory.

3. **Independence**. After Franklin was destroyed by the flood of 1828, the town of Independence became the major point of departure for merchants using the Santa Fe Trail. Several sites within today's Independence have a special relevance to the Trail, including the courthouse, the jail, and Woodlawn Cemetery.

4. **Westport Landing**. Now a part of greater Kansas City, Missouri, the town of Westport Landing, after succeeding Independence, became the last "official" beginning for the Santa Fe Trial. The Landing itself has been destroyed by commercial development, but the Old Westport Historic District contains many sites associated with the Trail's early history.

Kansas Sites

1. **Fort Leavenworth**. This large army post is not situated on the Santa Fe Trail. Its importance lies in the fact that it was from here that soldiers rode out to protect merchants on the Trail before the army built posts along the route especially for that purpose. Captain Bennet Riley and four companies of the 6th US Infantry Regiment departed

from here in 1829 to escort a large caravan of Missouri traders led by Charles Bent. Colonel Stephen Watts Kearny and his Army of the West also left from Fort Leavenworth in 1846 to occupy New Mexico and California for the United States.

2. **Santa Fe Trail / Oregon Trail Junction**. This is the point that the Oregon Trail separated from the Santa Fe Trail. The longer Oregon Trail was popular in the 1840s and later as an emigration route for thousands of Americans intent on settling the rich farmlands of the Pacific Northwest.

3. **Council Grove**. This small community was the place where individual westbound wagons rendezvoused before continuing their westward journeys on the Santa Fe Trail. Here, companies of wagons were formed, each with an elected captain. From this point on, the will of the majority was the order of the day. Sites associated with the Trail that can still be visited in Council Grove are the Post Office Oak, the Council Oak, the Last Chance Store, the Kaw Indian Mission, and the Hays House Restaurant.

4. **Fort Larned National Historic Site**. Among the forts located along the Santa Fe Trail, Fort Larned was surpassed in size only by Fort Union, New Mexico. Today, the fort is one of the best-preserved historic military facilities in America. Actual wagon-wheel ruts from freighting days on the Trail are located nearby.

5. **Fort Dodge**. Several buildings from the original fort survive. Today, the facility is the headquarters of the Kansas State Soldiers' Home.

OKLAHOMA SITE

1. **Camp Nichols**. Located on the Cimarron Cutoff, Camp Nichols was founded by Kit Carson in 1865. The fort's soldiers were responsible for protecting Trail merchants and travelers who had elected to take the somewhat shorter Cimarron Cutoff to Santa Fe. Marian Russell lived at the fort for a while.

COLORADO SITES

1. **Bent's Old Fort National Historic Site**. This structure is an exact reconstruction of the fort built by the Bent brothers and Ceran St. Vrain in the early 1830s. A visit here is like stepping back into yesteryear. The fort is meticulously furnished with relics from the days when the post was the foremost fur-trading facility on the southern Great Plains.

2. **Spanish Peaks**. These twin mountains can be seen for miles across the prairie. For weary merchants traveling the Santa Fe Trail, they served as a landmark signaling the approach to Raton Pass.

3. **Wootton Ranch**. Uncle Dick Wootton's ranch was located here at the northern entrance to Raton Pass.

NEW MEXICO SITES

1. **Raton Pass**. Today, Interstate Highway 25 glides smoothly and effortlessly over what used to be one of the most difficult sections of the Santa Fe Trail. After Uncle Dick Wootton completed his road improvements across the pass, many travelers who had previously preferred the Cimarron Cutoff reverted to using the Mountain Branch of the Santa Fe Trail.

2. **Rabbit Ears**. Located on the Cimarron Cutoff a few miles before it rejoins the main Santa Fe Trail, the Rabbit Ears are rock outcrops that to early passersby resembled a rabbit's ears.

3. **Wagon Mound**. This outcropping was the last major physical landmark on the Cimarron Cutoff. To some of the early merchants utilizing the Trail, the large mesa resembled a covered wagon.

4. **Fort Union National Monument**. The remains of what once was the largest military installation in the Southwest are still to be seen here. The site vividly depicts military life along the Santa Fe Trail from the 1860s to the 1880s.

5. **Las Vegas**. This town was established in 1835, well after the Santa Fe Trail had become a frequently used thoroughfare. The village's plaza was built right around the old Trail. In addition to its Trail history, Las Vegas provides an interesting look at late-nineteenth-century New Mexican architecture.

6. **Pecos National Historical Park**. The abandoned pueblo and old Spanish church conjure up visions of life among the Indians more than three hundred years ago. A beautiful museum and a walking tour around the pueblo go a long way toward making a visit here memorable, indeed.

7. **Glorieta Battlefield**. One of the most important engagements during the Civil War in the Trans-Mississippi Theater was fought here in March 1862. Sometimes called "the Gettysburg of the West," the defeat of Confederate forces here put New Mexico into the hands of Union authorities for the duration of the conflict.

8. **Santa Fe**. Beginning with the Plaza, which represented the westernmost point on the Santa Fe Trail, one has little difficulty finding many points of historical interest in this fascinating town. Trail-related sites include the Palace of the Governors, the site of Fort Marcy, and a long section of the Trail itself which approaches Santa Fe from the south.

These points of interest are only a few of the many sites that can still be seen along the Santa Fe Trail today. Although the sights and sounds of the old Trail are gone forever, it is good that these reminders of the past still provide vivid insights into what life was really like on the Trail during its golden years.

Appendix A

Chronology of Important Events in the Evolution and Development of the Santa Fe Trail

1492 Christopher Columbus, a Genoese explorer sailing for Spain, lands in the West Indies on October 12, thus laying Spanish claim to practically all of the Western Hemisphere.

1519 Hernán Cortés sails from Cuba for Mexico, lands there on March 4, and establishes a colony which he calls Veracruz.

1521 Cortés begins the final assault upon the Aztec capital of Tenochtitlan in May, and on August 13 he enters the city as the conqueror of Mexico.

1540 Francisco de Coronado leaves Compostela, Mexico, in February and, for the next two years, explores much of the American Southwest, including the Pueblo town of Pecos.

1590 Gaspar Castaño de Sosa attempts to establish a colony in New Mexico. With thirty-seven companions, he visits Pecos Pueblo on December 31.

1598 Juan de Oñate leads a colony of Spanish soldiers and priests into New Mexico. On April 30 he claims for Spain all of the land drained by the Rio Grande.

1610 New Mexico's governor, Pedro de Peralta, establishes the town of Santa Fe in the spring.

1625 Spanish priests complete the first church at Pecos Pueblo. It is called the Mission of our Lady of the Angels of Porciuncula.

1680 Inhabitants of several Pueblo towns in northern New Mexico, including Pecos, revolt against the Spanish and drive their masters back to Mexico. The church at Pecos is destroyed.

1692 Don Diego de Vargas re-conquers New Mexico for Spain. The Pueblo Revolt is officially over.

1717 Fray José de Arranegui rebuilds the church at Pecos with less-elaborate dimensions.

1739 The Mallet brothers, Paul and Peter, along with several other French companions, reach Santa Fe on July 22.

1792 Pedro Vial leaves Santa Fe in May for St. Louis on what becomes the first documented trip across the Santa Fe Trail.

1804 Kaskaskia merchant William Morrison sends Jeannot Metoyer and Baptiste LaLande to Santa Fe on a trading mission. Lorenzo Durocher and Jacques d'Eglise follow sometime later.

1805 James Purcell, a Kentucky fur trapper, arrives in Santa Fe, decides to permanently relocate there, and becomes a carpenter in the Spanish town.

1807 In March, Lieutenant Zebulon Pike enters Santa Fe as a prisoner of Spanish soldiers. Pike is later released unharmed. In December, Jacques Clamorgan, a St. Louis trader, visits Santa Fe.

1808 Fort Osage, perched on a high bluff overlooking the Missouri River, is completed. It is officially named on November 10.

1812 The Robert McKnight trading party leaves the Missouri settlements for Santa Fe. Upon arrival there, the men are jailed, and some of them are held until 1821. Missouri Territory is organized on June 4.

1821 During this momentous year in Santa Fe Trail history, Missouri becomes the nation's twenty-fourth state on August 10. On September 27 Mexico declares its independence from Spain. William Becknell leaves Franklin, Missouri, in September, follows the Santa Fe Trail, and reaches Santa Fe on November 16, only two weeks before another trading party led by John McKnight.

1822 With three loaded wagons, William Becknell starts out on another trading mission in late May. He establishes the "Cimarron Cutoff" as a viable alternative to the "Mountain Route" of the Santa Fe Trail.

1825 On March 3 President James Monroe signs legislation authorizing the survey of the Santa Fe Trail. The survey party leaves Fort Osage on July 17.

1827 Fort Leavenworth is built. Its primary purpose is to provide military troops for the protection of American merchants and travelers who use the Santa Fe Trail.

1828 The value of goods freighted down the Santa Fe Trail exceeds $100,000 for the first time. The eastern terminus of the Trail moves to Independence, Missouri, after Franklin is washed away by the Missouri River.

1829 Major Bennet Riley and four companies of the US 6th Infantry leave Fort Leavenworth and escort a caravan of Missouri traders along the Santa Fe Trail to the Arkansas River, then the border between Mexico and the United States.

1831 Jedediah Smith, the noted American mountain man, trying his hand at the Santa Fe trade for the first time, is killed by Indians on the Trail near the Cimarron River on May 27. Also, in May, Josiah Gregg leaves Independence on the first of many trips to Santa Fe.

1833 Mary Donoho, the first Anglo-American woman to travel the Santa Fe Trail, arrives in the capital city in August. Bent's Fort, located on the Trail near its crossing of the Arkansas River, is completed.

1835 The town of Las Vegas is founded along the Santa Fe Trail in New Mexico.

1838 The last residents of Pecos Pueblo move to join kinsmen at Jemez Pueblo.

1843 In April, prominent Mexican merchant Antonio José Chávez is robbed and murdered on the Santa Fe Trail by Texas ruffians.

1844 Josiah Gregg's classic, *Commerce of the Prairies*, is published in New York in July.

1845 The United States annexes Texas in March.

1846 On May 13 the United States and Mexico go to war over the Texas annexation issue. Colonel Stephen Watts Kearny departs Fort Leavenworth on June 16 with his Army of the West to occupy New Mexico and California. Susan Shelby Magoffin leaves Independence in early June for a trip to Santa Fe with her husband. They arrive on August 31.

1847 An uprising of dissident Indians and Mexicans in Taos on January 19 casts a pall over Kearny's peaceful occupation of New Mexico. Charles Bent, the newly appointed governor of the territory, and several other Americans and Mexican loyalists are murdered during the melee.

1849 William Bent, disheartened by the paltry price that the US Army offers him for Bent's Fort, blows up the structure and moves a few miles down the Arkansas River.

1850 Josiah Gregg dies in California in February. New Mexico Territory is created on September 9.

1851 Construction begins on Fort Union, located in New Mexico at the junction of the Cimarron Cutoff and the Mountain Branch of the Santa Fe Trail.

1852 Marion Mahoney (Russell) leaves Westport Landing for Santa Fe.

1854 Kansas Territory is created on May 30.

1856 William Becknell dies on April 25.

1859 Fort Larned in Kansas is built to protect the eastern end of the Santa Fe Trail.

1861 On January 29 Kansas is admitted to the Union as the thirty-fourth state. Colorado Territory is established on February 28.

1862 Confederate and Union forces clash at the decisive Battle of Glorieta Pass in late March. The Confederate defeat sends the Southerners back to Texas and leaves New Mexico in the hands of Union authorities.

1863 The third and final version of Fort Union is begun. When it is completed, the post will be the largest and most important army facility in the Southwest. Ernestine Huling travels the Santa Fe Trail.

1864 Fort Dodge is built in Kansas near the forks of the Santa Fe Trail. The noted cowtown Dodge City will one day blossom nearby.

1865 Camp Nichols, located on the Cimarron Cutoff in today's state of Oklahoma, is established by Kit Carson.

1866 Majors, Russell, and Waddell, the largest freighting company operating on the Santa Fe Trail, hauls 16 million pounds of freight this year. The firm employs 5,000 men and utilizes 3,500 wagons, 40,000 oxen, and 1,000 mules. Uncle Dick Wootton begins work on his toll road across Raton Pass.

1876 The Atchison, Topeka and Santa Fe Railway reaches Pueblo, Colorado. Colorado becomes the nation's thirty-eighth state on August 1.

1878 Fort Larned is abandoned.

1879 The railroad reaches Las Vegas, New Mexico, in July.

1880 On February 9 the first train of the Atchison, Topeka and Santa Fe Railway steams into Santa Fe by way of a spur track from the village of Lamy. For all practical purposes, the Santa Fe Trail is now "out of business."

1882 Fort Dodge is abandoned.

1890 Oklahoma Territory is established on May 2.

1891 Fort Union is abandoned.

1907 Oklahoma becomes the nation's forty-sixth state on November 16.

1912 New Mexico becomes the nation's forty-seventh state on January 6.

1915 The American archaeologist Alfred V. Kidder begins the first scientifically organized excavation at Pecos.

1964 Hollywood legend Greer Garson and her husband, Colonel E. F. Fogelson, donate 279 acres of their Forked Lightning Ranch as a buffer zone around the Pecos Pueblo ruins.

1965 Legislation is passed by Congress that authorizes the establishment of Pecos National Monument, today called Pecos National Historical Park.

1987 The Santa Fe National Historic Trail is designated part of the National Trail System.

1990 The US Congress passes legislation to protect Forked Lightning Ranch as part of the newly recommended Pecos National Historical Park.

1991 Greer Garson sells the nearly six-thousand-acre Forked Lightning Ranch to the Conservation Fund, which in turn donates the property to the National Park Service.

Appendix B

General Stephen Watts Kearny's Speech to the Citizens of Las Vegas

Mr. Alcade [the mayor] and the people of New Mexico: I have come amongst you by the orders of my government, to take possession of your country, and extend over it the laws of the United States. We consider it, and have done so for some time, a part of the territory of the United States. We come amongst you as friends—not as enemies; as protectors—not as conquerors. We come among you for your benefit—not for your injury.

Henceforth, I absolve you from all allegiance to the Mexican government, and from all obedience to General Armijo. He is no longer your governor; I am your governor. I shall not expect you to take up arms and follow me, to fight your own people who may oppose me; but I now tell you, that those who remain peaceably at home, attending to their crops and their herds, shall be protected by me in their property, their persons, and their religion; and not a pepper, nor an onion, shall be disturbed or taken by my troops without pay, or without the consent of the owner. But listen! he who promises to be quiet, and is found in arms against me, I will hang.

From the Mexican government you have never received protection. The Apaches and Navajhoes [*sic*] come down from the mountains and carry off your sheep, and even your women, whenever they please. My government will correct all this. It will keep off the Indians, protect you in your persons and property; and, I repeat again, will protect you in your religion. I know you are all great Catholics; that some of your priests have told you all sorts of stories—that we should ill-treat your women, and brand them on the cheek as you do your mules on the hip. It is all false. My government respects your religion as much as the Protestant religion, and allows each man to worship his Creator as his heart tells him is best. Its laws protect the Catholic as well as the Protestant; the weak as well as the strong; the poor as well as the rich. I am not a Catholic myself—I was not brought up in that faith; but at least one-third of my army are Catholics, and I respect a good Catholic as much as a good Protestant.

There goes my army—you see but a small portion of it; there are many more behind—resistance is useless.

Mr. Alcade, and you two captains of militia, the laws of my country require that all men who hold office under it shall take the oath of allegiance. I do not wish for the present, until affairs become more settled, to disturb your form of government. If you are prepared to take oaths of allegiance, I shall continue you in office and support your authority.

Source: William H. Emory, *Notes of a Military Reconnoissance,[sic] from Fort Leavenworth, in Missouri, to San Diego, in California, Including Part of the Arkansas, Del Norte, and Gila Rivers* (Washington, DC: Wendell and Van Benthuysen, Printers, 1848), Executive Document 41, pp. 27–28.

Appendix C

General Stephen Watts Kearny's Proclamation to the Citizens of Santa Fe

As by the act of the republic of Mexico, a state of war exists between that government and the United States; and as the undersigned, at the head of his troops, on the 18th instant, took possession of Santa Fe, the capital of the department of New Mexico, he now announces his intention to hold the department, with its original boundaries (on both sides of the Del Norte), as part of the United States, and under the name of "the Territory of New Mexico."

The undersigned has come to New Mexico with a strong military force, and an equally strong one is following close in his rear. He has more troops than necessary to put down any opposition that can possibly be brought against him, and therefore it would be but folly or madness for any dissatisfied or discontented persons to think of resisting him.

The undersigned has instructions from his government to respect the religious institutions of New Mexico—to protect the property of the church—to cause the worship of those belonging to it to be undisturbed, and their religious rights in the implicit manner preserved to them—also to protect the persons and property of all quiet and peaceable inhabitants within its boundaries against their enemies, the Eutaws [*sic*], the Navajoes [*sic*], and others; and when he assures all that it will be his pleasure, as well as his duty, to comply with those instructions, he calls upon them to exert themselves in preserving order, in promoting concord, and in maintaining the authority and efficacy of the laws. And he requires of those who have left their homes and taken up arms against the troops of the United States to return forthwith to them, or else they will be considered as enemies and traitors, subjecting their persons to punishments and their property to seizure and confiscation for the benefit of the public treasury.

It is the wish and intention of the United States to provide for New Mexico a free government, with the least possible delay, similar to those in the United States; and the people of New Mexico will then be called on to exercise the rights of freemen in electing their own representatives to the Territorial legislature. But until this can be done, the laws hitherto in existence will be continued until changed or modified by competent authority; and those persons holding office will continue in the same for the present, provided they will consider themselves good citizens and are willing to take the oath of allegiance to the United States.

The United States hereby absolves all persons residing within the boundaries of New Mexico from any further allegiance to the republic of Mexico, and hereby claims them as citizens of the United States. Those who remain quiet and peaceable will be considered good citizens and receive protection—those who are found in arms, or instigating others against the United States, will be considered as traitors, and treated accordingly.

Don Manuel Armijo, the late governor of this department, has fled from it: the undersigned has taken possession of it without firing a gun, or spilling a single drop of blood, in which he truly rejoices, and for the present will be considered as governor of the Territory.

Source: James K. Polk, *Occupation of Mexican Territory: Message from the President of the United States* (Washington, DC: 1846), 29th Congress, 2nd Session, Executive Document 19, pp. 20–21.

Appendix D

Josiah Gregg's Table of Distances between Independence, Missouri, and Santa Fe, New Mexico

From Independence to:	Miles	Aggregate
Round Grove	35	
Narrows	30	65
110-Mile Creek	35	100
Bridge Creek	8	108
Big John Springs (crossing several creeks)	40	148
Council Grove	2	150
Diamond Spring	15	165
Lost Spring	15	180
Cottonwood Creek	12	192
Turkey Creek	25	217
Little Arkansas River	17	234
Cow Creek	20	254
Arkansas River	16	270
Walnut Creek (up Arkansas River)	8	278
Ash Creek	19	297
Pawnee Fork	6	303
Coon Creek	33	336
Caches	36	372
Ford of Arkansas	20	392
Sand Creek (leave Arkansas River)	50	442
Cimarron River (Lower Spring)	8	450
Middle Spring (up Cimarron River)	36	486
Willow Bar	26	512
Upper Spring	18	530

From Independence to:	Miles	Aggregate
Cold Spring (leave Cimarron River)	5	535
M'Nees Crossing	25	560
Rabbit-Ears Creek	20	580
Round Mound	8	588
Rock Creek	8	596
Point of Rocks	19	615
Rio Colorado	20	635
Ocatè	6	641
Santa Clara Spring	21	662
Rio Mora	22	684
Rio Gallinas (Vegas)	20	704
Ojo de Bernal (spring)	17	721
San Miguel	6	727
Pecos village	23	750
Santa Fe	25	775

Appendix E

Josiah Gregg's Table of Santa Fe Trade Statistics

Years	Value of Merchandise (US dollars)	Number of Wagons	Number of Men	Remarks
1822	15,000		70	Pack animals only used
1823	12,000		50	Pack animals only used
1824	35,000	26	100	Pack animals and wagons used
1825	65,000	37	130	Pack animals and wagons used
1826	90,000	60	100	Henceforth, only wagons used
1827	85,000	55	90	
1828	150,000	100	200	Three men killed
1829	60,000	30	50	First US Army escort used; one trader killed
1830	120,000	70	140	First oxen used by traders
1831	250,000	130	320	Two men killed
1832	140,000	70	150	Party defeated on
1833	180,000	105	185	Canadian River; two men killed, three perished
1834	150,000	80	160	Second army escort
1835	140,000	75	140	
1836	130,000	70	135	
1837	150,000	80	160	
1838	90,000	50	100	

Years	Value of Merchandise (US dollars)	Number of Wagons	Number of Men	Remarks
1839	250,000	130	250	Arkansas Expedition
1840	50,000	30	60	Chihuahua Expedition
1841	150,000	60	100	Texan Santa Fe Expedition
1842	160,000	70	120	
1843	450,000	230	350	Third army escort; ports closed

ENDNOTES

CHAPTER ONE: BEFORE THE SANTA FE TRAIL WAS A TRAIL

1. Quoted in John L. Kessell, *Kiva, Cross, and Crown* (Washington, DC: National Park Service, 1979), pp. 8–9, from Pedro Castañeda, *Relacion del la Jornada de Cibola, etc.*, translated in George Parker Winship, "The Coronado Expedition, 1540–1542," in *Fourteenth Annual Report*, Bureau of American Ethnology (Washington, DC: Government Printing Office, 1896).

2. David Grant Noble, "Pecos Pueblo, December 31, 1590," in *Exploration* (Santa Fe: School of American Research, 1981), p. 27, from the translation of Gaspar Castaño de Sosa's journals by Albert H. Schroeder and Dan S. Matson (Santa Fe: School of American Research, 1965).

3. Attributed to Francisco Vázquez de Coronado. Quoted in Tom McHugh, *The Time of the Buffalo* (New York: Alfred A. Knopf, 1972), p. 13.

4. Josiah Gregg, *Commerce of the Prairies* (New York: Henry G. Langley, 1844), vol. 2, p. 212.

5. Quoted in George E. Hyde, *Life of George Bent Written from his Letters* (Norman: University of Oklahoma Press, 1968), p. 18.

6. Ibid., p. 35.

7. Gregg, *Commerce of the Prairies*, vol. 2, p. 228.

8. Ibid., p. 230.

CHAPTER TWO: THE LURE OF SANTA FE

1. Quoted in Noel M. Loomis and Abraham P. Nasatir, *Pedro Vial and the Roads to Santa Fe* (Norman: University of Oklahoma Press, 1967), p. 390.

2. Zebulon Montgomery Pike, *An Account of Expeditions to the Sources of the Mississippi, and Through the Western Parts of Louisiana, to the Sources of the Arkansaw, Kans, La Latte, and Pierre Jaun, Rivers, etc.* (Philadelphia: C. & A. Conrad & Company, 1810), Appendix to Part III, p. 41.

3. Ibid., p. 212.

4. Ibid., p. 217.

5. Ibid., pp. 212–14.

6. Ibid., pp. 215–16.

7. Ibid., pp. 217–18.

8. Quoted in William H. Goetzmann, *Exploration and Empire* (Austin: Texas State Historical Association, 1993), p. 51, from Zebulon M. Pike, *The Expeditions of Zebulon Montgomery Pike,* Elliott Cous, editor (New York: 1895).

9. John C. Luttig, *Journal of a Fur-Trading Expedition on the Upper Missouri 1812–1813* (New York: Argosy-Antiquarian Ltd., 1964), pp. 142–43.

10. *American State Papers,* Foreign Relations, Volume IV (Washington, DC: Gales and Seaton, 1834), p. 211.

11. Ibid., p. 213.

12. David Meriwether, *My Life in the Mountains and on the Plains* (Norman: University of Oklahoma Press, 1965), p. 89.

13. Ibid.

14. Ibid., p. 92.

CHAPTER THREE: TRAILS WEST!

1. Quoted in Larry M. Beachum, *William Becknell: Father of the Santa Fe Trade* (El Paso: Texas Western Press, 1982), p. 17, from the Franklin *Missouri Intelligencer,* June 25, 1821, p. 3.

2. Ibid., p. 28, from the Franklin *Missouri Intelligencer*, April 22, 1823, p. 2.

3. Ibid., pp. 28–29, from the Franklin *Missouri Intelligencer*, April 22, 1823, p. 2.

4. Ibid., p. 29, from the Franklin *Missouri Intelligencer*, April 22, 1823, p. 2.

5. Ibid., pp. 30–31, from the Franklin *Missouri Intelligencer*, April 22, 1823, p. 2.

6. Ibid., p. 32, from Robert L. Duffus, *The Santa Fe Trail* (New York: Longmans, Green & Company, 1930).

7. Ibid., p. 34, from the Franklin *Missouri Intelligencer*, April 22, 1823, p. 2.

8. Gregg, *Commerce of the Prairies,* vol. 1, pp. 22–23.

9. Beachum, *William Becknell: Father of the Santa Fe Trade,* p. 38, from the Franklin *Missouri Intelligencer,* April 22, 1823, p. 2.

10. Ibid., p. 42, from the Franklin *Missouri Intelligencer,* June 25, 1823, p. 3.

CHAPTER FOUR: SURVEYING THE TRAIL

1. Thomas Hart Benton, *Thirty Years' View, or, a History of the Working of the American Government for Thirty Years, from 1820 to 1850* (New York: D. Appleton and Company, 1854), vol. 1, pp. 41–44.

2. Kate L. Gregg, ed., *The Road to Santa Fe: The Journal and Diaries of George Champlin Sibley* (Albuquerque, NM: University of New Mexico Press, 1995), p. 17.

3. Ibid., p. 30.

4. Ibid., pp. 32–33.

5. Ibid., p. 83.

6. Ibid, pp. 204–05.

CHAPTER FIVE: FREIGHTING ON THE SANTA FE TRAIL

1. Captain R. B. Marcy, *The Prairie and Overland Traveller* (London: Sampson Low, Son, and Co., 1860), pp. 8–11.

2. Gregg, *Commerce of the Prairies,* vol. 1, p. 49.

3. Ibid., pp. 110–11.

Chapter Six: The First Military Escort on the Santa Fe Trail

1. Gregg, *Commerce of the Prairies,* vol. 1, p. 28.

2. *American State Papers,* Indian Affairs, Volume II (Washington, DC: Gales and Seaton, 1834), p. 452.

3. Quoted in Otis E. Young, *The First Military Escort on the Santa Fe Trail 1829* (Glendale, CA: Arthur H. Clark Company, 1952), p. 179.

4. Ibid., p. 100, from Philip St. George Cooke, *Scenes and Adventures in the Army* (Philadelphia, 1859), pp. 48–49.

5. Ibid., pp. 186, 188.

6. Ibid., pp. 190–91.

7. Ibid., p. 123, from Cooke, *Scenes and Adventures,* p. 56.

Chapter Seven: Bent's Fort

1. John E. Sunder, ed., *Matt Field on the Santa Fe Trail* (Norman: University of Oklahoma Press, 1960), pp. 44–45.

2. George Frederick Ruxton, *Life in the Far West,* Leroy R. Hafen, ed. (Norman: University of Oklahoma Press, 1951), pp. 179–81.

3. James William Abert, *Report of an Expedition Led by Lieutenant Abert, on the Upper Arkansas and through the Country of the Comanche Indians, in the Fall of the Year 1845* (Washington, DC: 29th Congress, 1st Session, Senate Document No. 438, 1846), p. 2.

Chapter Eight: Women on the Santa Fe Trail

1. Quoted in Marian Meyer, *Mary Donoho: New First Lady of the Santa Fe Trail* (Santa Fe: Ancient City Press, 1991), p. 37, from W. H. H. Allison, "Santa Fe as It Appeared During the Winter of the Years 1837 and 1838," *Old Santa Fe* (1914), pp. 176–77.

2. Ibid., pp. 51–52, from Allison, *Old Santa Fe,* pp. 178–79.

3. Ibid., pp. 67–69, from *The Rachael Plummer Narrative* (N.p.: Rachel Lofton, Susie Hendrix and Jane Kennedy, 1926), p. 116.

4. E. House, *A Narrative of the Captivity of Mrs. Horn, and Her Two Children, with Mrs. Harris, by the Camanche Indians, etc.* (St. Louis: C. Keemle, Printer, 1839), p. 52.

5. Stella M. Drumm, ed., *Down the Santa Fe Trail and into Mexico: The Diary of Susan Shelby Magoffin 1846–1847* (Lincoln: University of Nebraska Press, 1982), p. 2.

6. Ibid, p. 66.

7. Ibid., p. 80.

8. Ibid. p. 102.

9. Ibid., pp. 114–15.

10. Franz Huning, *Trader on the Santa Fe Trail: The Memoirs of Franz Huning* (Albuquerque, NM: The University of Albuquerque, 1973), pp. 94–95.

11. Ibid., p. 95.

12. Ibid.

CHAPTER NINE: JOSIAH GREGG

1. Gregg, *Commerce of the Prairies*, vol. 1, pp. 143–44.
2. Ibid., vol. 2, p. 213.
3. Ibid., pp. 167–68.
4. See Appendix D for a complete listing of Gregg's distances along the Santa Fe Trail.
5. See Appendix E for a complete listing of Gregg's statistics of the Santa Fe trade for the years 1822–1843.

CHAPTER TEN: THE ARMY OF THE WEST

1. Gregory J. W. Urwin, *The United States Cavalry: An Illustrated History* (Poole, Dorset, UK: Blandford Press, 1983), p. 56.
2. Ralph P. Bieber, ed., *Marching with the Army of the West, 1846–1848* (Philadelphia: Porcupine Press, 1974), pp. 23–24.
3. Allan Nevins, ed., *Polk: The Diary of a President, 1845–1849* (New York: Longmans, Green and Company, 1952), p. 107.
4. Ibid.
5. Ibid.
6. James K. Polk, *Occupation of Mexican Territory. Message from the President of the United States* (Washington, DC, 1846) 29th Congress, 2nd Session, Executive Document 19, p. 5.
7. Ibid.
8. Ibid., p. 6
9. John T. Hughes, *Doniphan's Expedition; Containing an Account of the Conquest of New Mexico* (Cincinnati: J. A. & U. P. James, 1850), pp. 25–26.
10. Ibid. p., 32.
11. Abraham Robinson Johnston, *Journal of Abraham Robinson Johnston*, in Bieber, ed., *Marching with the Army of the West*, p. 88
12. Ibid., p. 89.
13. Hughes, *Doniphan's Expedition*, p. 47.
14. Ibid., p. 56.
15. Polk, *Occupation of Mexican Territory*, p. 19.
16. William H. Emory, *Notes of a Military Reconnoissance [sic], from Fort Leavenworth, in Missouri, to San Diego in California, Including Part of the Arkansas, Del Norte, and Gila Rivers* (Washington, DC: Wendell and Van Benthuysen, Printers, 1848), Executive Document 41, p. 18.
17. James W. Abert, *Report of Lieut. J. W. Abert, of His Examination of New Mexico, in the Years 1846–47* (Washington, DC, 1848), 30th Congress, 1st Session, Executive Document 23, p. 25.
18. Ralph Emerson Twitchell, *The History of the Military Occupation of the Territory of New Mexico from 1846 to 1851* (Denver: Smith-Brooks Company, Publishers, 1909), pp. 60–63.
19. Emory, *Notes of a Military Reconnoissance*, p. 21.
20. Ibid., pp. 21–22.

21. Ibid., p. 23.

22. Ibid., pp. 25–26.

23. See Appendix B for the full text of Kearny's speech.

24. Emory, *Notes of a Military Reconnoissance*, p. 29.

25. Drumm, ed., *Down the Santa Fe Trail and into Mexico*, p. xxiv, from Milo M. Quaife, *The Diary of James K. Polk during His Presidency, 1845 to 1849* (Chicago, 1910), p. 474.

26. Thomas Hart Benton, *Thirty Years' View*, vol. 2, p. 683.

27. For excellent coverage regarding the events surrounding the secret meetings between the American agent, Magoffin, and Mexican authorities, see the passages about the incident in the following: Bernard De Voto, *The Year of Decision: 1846* (New York: Book-of-the-Month Club, 1984); Paul Horgan, *Great River: The Rio Grande in North American History* (New York: Rinehart & Company, 1954); and David Lavender, *Bent's Fort* (Garden City, NY: Doubleday & Company, 1954).

28. Emory, *Notes of a Military Reconnoissance*, pp. 30–31.

29. Ibid., p. 31.

30. Ibid., p. 32.

31. Ibid., pp. 34–35.

32. Abert, *Report of Lieut. J. W. Abert*, p. 32.

33. Hughes, *Doniphan's Expedition*, p. 91.

34. Twitchell, *The History of the Military Occupation of New Mexico, 1846–1851*, p. 75.

35. *Emory Notes of a Military Reconnoissance*, p. 33.

36. Ibid.

37. See Appendix C for the full text of Kearny's proclamation.

38. Polk, *Occupation of Mexican Territory*, p. 21.

CHAPTER ELEVEN: THE SANTA FE TRAIL DURING THE 1850S AND 1860S

1. Quoted in Robert M. Utley, "Fort Union National Monument–New Mexico" (Washington, DC: National Park Service, US Department of the Interior, 1962), p. 9.

2. Mrs. Orsemus B. Boyd, 1894, quoted in Utley, "Fort Union National Monument–New Mexico."

3. Utley, *Fort Union*, pp. 10–11.

4. Ibid., p. 59.

5. Howard Louis Conard, *"Uncle Dick" Wootton* (Chicago: W. E. Dibble & Co., 1890), pp. 417–18.

6. Ibid., p. 419.

7. Ibid.

8. Ibid., p. 420.

9. Ibid., p. 421.

Selected Bibliography

Abert, James W. *Report of an Expedition Led by Lieutenant Abert, on the Upper Arkansas and through the Country of the Comanche Indians, in the Fall of the Year 1845.* Washington, DC: 29th Congress, 1st Session, 1846. Senate Document No. 438.

———. *Report of Lieut. J. W. Abert, of His Examination of New Mexico, in the Years 1846–47.* Washington, DC: 30th Congress, 1st Session, 1848. Executive Document 23.

American State Papers. Indian Affairs, Volume II. Washington, DC: Gales and Seaton, 1834.

———. Foreign Relations, Volume IV. Washington, DC: Gales and Seaton, 1834.

Barry, Louise. *The Beginnings of the West.* Topeka: Kansas State Historical Society, 1972.

Barsness, Larry. *The Bison in Art.* Flagstaff, AZ: Northland Press, 1977.

Beachum, Larry M. *William Becknell: Father of the Santa Fe Trade.* El Paso: Texas Western Press, 1982.

Benton, Thomas Hart. *Thirty Years' View; or, A History of the Working of the American Government for Thirty Years, from 1820 to 1850.* New York: D. Appleton and Company, 1854.

Bent's Fort on the Arkansas. Denver: State Historical Society of Colorado, 1954.

Bent's Old Fort. Denver: State Historical Society of Colorado, 1979.

Bezy, John V., and Joseph P. Sanchez, ed. *Pecos: Gateway to Pueblo and Plains: The Anthology.* Tucson: Southwest Parks & Monuments Association, 1988.

Bieber, Ralph P., ed. *Marching with the Army of the West, 1846–1848.* Philadelphia: Porcupine Press, 1974.

Brown, William E. *The Santa Fe Trail.* St. Louis: Patrice Press, 1988.

Chittenden, Hiram Martin. *The American Fur Trade of the Far West.* New York: Francis P. Harper, 1902.

Conard, Howard Louis. *"Uncle Dick" Wootton.* Chicago: W. E. Dibble & Company, 1890.

Cooke, Philip St. George. *The Conquest of New Mexico and California.* Chicago: Rio Grande Press, 1964.

Crutchfield, James A. "Marching with the Army of the West," in *Black Powder Annual.* Union City, TN: Dixie Gun Works, 1991.

———. Revolt at Taos: The New Mexican and Indian Insurrection of 1847. Yardley PA: Westholme, 2015.

Day, A. Grove. *Coronado's Quest.* Berkeley: University of California Press, 1964.

Dorian, Edith, and W. N. Wilson. *Trails West, and Men Who Made Them*. New York: Whittlesey House, 1955.

Driggs, Howard R. *The Old West Speaks*. Englewood Cliffs, NJ: Prentice-Hall, 1956.

Drumm, Stella M., ed. *Down the Santa Fe Trail and Into Mexico: The Diary of Susan Shelby Magoffin, 1846–1847*. Lincoln: University of Nebraska Press, 1982.

Eggenhofer, Nick. *Wagons, Mules, and Men*. New York: Hastings House Publishers, 1961.

Emory, W. H. *Notes of a Military Reconnoissance [sic], from Fort Leavenworth, Missouri, to San Diego, in California, Including Part of the Arkansas, Del Norte, and Gila Rivers*. Washington, DC: 30th Congress, 1st Session, 1848. Executive Document 41.

Fowler, Jacob. *The Journal of Jacob Fowler*. Minneapolis: Ross & Haines, 1965.

Galvin, John, ed., *Western America in 1846–1847: The Original Travel Diary of Lieutenant J. W. Abert*. San Francisco: John Howell-Books, 1966.

Garrard, Lewis H. *Wah-to-yah and the Taos Trail*. Norman: University of Oklahoma Press, 1955.

Goetzmann, William H. *Exploration and Empire*. Austin: Texas State Historical Association, 1993.

Gregg, Josiah. *Commerce of the Prairies, or the Journal of a Santa Fe Trader, during Eight Expeditions across the Great Western Prairies, and a Residence of Nearly Nine Years in Northern Mexico*. New York: Henry G. Langley, 1844.

———. *Commerce of the Prairies*. Max L. Moorhead, ed. Norman: University of Oklahoma Press, 1954.

Gregg, Kate L., ed. *The Road to Santa Fe: The Journal and Diaries of George Champlin Sibley*. Albuquerque, NM: University of New Mexico Press, 1995.

Henritze, Cosette, and Jane Kurtz. *The Santa Fe Trail: Dangers and Dollars*. Trinidad, CO: Roots and Wings Publishing, 1987.

Hill, William E. *The Santa Fe Trail, Yesterday and Today*. Caldwell, ID: Caxton Printers, 1992.

Holling, Holling C. *Tree in the Trail*. Boston: Houghton Mifflin Company, 1970.

House, E. *A Narrative of the Captivity of Mrs. Horn, and Her Two Children, with Mrs. Harris, by the Camanche Indians, etc.* St. Louis: C. Keemle, Printer, 1839.

Hughes, John T. *Doniphan's Expedition; Containing an Account of the Conquest of New Mexico*. Cincinnati: J. A. & U. P. James, 1850.

Huning, Franz. *Trader on the Santa Fe Trail: The Memoirs of Franz Huning*. Albuquerque, NM: University of Albuquerque Press, 1973.

Hyde, George E. *Life of George Bent Written from his Letters*. Norman: University of Oklahoma Press, 1968.

James, H. L. *The Santa Fe Trail*. N.p., 1984.

James, Thomas. *Three Years among the Indians and Mexicans*. New York: The Citadel Press, 1966.

Kendall, George Wilkins. *Narrative of the Texan Santa Fe Expedition*. New York: Harper and Brothers, 1844.

Kessell, John L. *Kiva, Cross, and Crown*. Washington, DC: National Park Service, 1979.

Lavender, David. *Bent's Fort*. Garden City, NY: Doubleday & Company, 1954.

———. *The Trail to Santa Fe*. Santa Fe: Trails West Publishing, 1989.

Loomis, Noel M., and Abraham P. Nasatir. *Pedro Vial and the Roads to Santa Fe*. Norman: University of Oklahoma Press, 1967.

Luttig, John C. *Journal of a Fur-Trading Expedition on the Upper Missouri, 1812–1813*. New York: Argosy-Antiquarian Ltd., 1964.

Marcy, Captain R. B. *The Prairie and Overland Traveller*. London: Sampson Low, Son, and Co., 1860.

Martin, Gene, and Mary Martin. *Trail Dust: A Quick Picture History of the Santa Fe Trail*. Manitou Springs, CO: Martin Associates, 1972.

McHugh, Tom. *The Time of the Buffalo*. New York: Alfred A. Knopf, 1972.

Meriwether, David. *My Life in the Mountains and on the Plains*. Norman: University of Oklahoma Press, 1965.

Meyer, Marian. *Mary Donoho: New First Lady of the Santa Fe Trail*. Santa Fe: Ancient City Press, 1991.

Mumey, Nolie. *Old Forts and Trading Posts of the West*. Denver: Artcraft Press, 1956.

Napton, W. B. *On the Santa Fe Trail in 1857*. Arrow Rock, MO: Friends of Arrow Rock, 1991.

Nevins, Allan, ed. *Polk: The Diary of a President, 1845–1849*. New York: Longmans, Green and Company, 1952.

Noble, David Grant. "Pecos Pueblo, December 31, 1590," in *Exploration*. Santa Fe: School of American Research, 1981.

———. *Santa Fe: History of an Ancient City*. Santa Fe: School of American Research, 1989.

Oglesby, Richard Edward. *Manuel Lisa and the Opening of the Missouri Fur Trade*. Norman: University of Oklahoma Press, 1963.

Oliva, Leo E. *Soldiers on the Santa Fe Trail*. Norman: University of Oklahoma Press. 1967.

Pike, Zebulon Montgomery. *An Account of Expeditions to the Sources of the Mississippi, and Through the Western Parts of Louisiana, to the Sources of the Arkansaw, Kans, La Platte, and Pierre Jaun Rivers, etc.* Philadelphia: C & A Conrad & Company, 1810.

Polk, James K. *Occupation of Mexican Territory*. Message from the President of the United States. Washington, DC: 29th Congress, 2nd Session, 1846. Executive Document 19.

Rittenhouse, Jack D. *The Santa Fe Trail: A Historical Bibliography*. Albuquerque, NM: Jack D. Rittenhouse, 1986.

Ruxton, George Frederick. Leroy R. Hafen, ed. *Life in the Far West*. Norman: University of Oklahoma Press, 1951.

Schubert, Frank N. *Vanguard of Expansion: Army Engineers in the Trans-Mississippi West, 1819–1879*. Washington, DC: Historical Division, Office of Administrative Services, Office of the Chief of Engineers, United States Army, n.d.

Simmons, Marc. *Following the Santa Fe Trail: A Guide for Modern Travelers*. Santa Fe: Ancient City Press, 1984.

Sunder, John E. *Matt Field on the Santa Fe Trail*. Norman: University of Oklahoma Press, 1960.

Terrell, John Upton. *American Indian Almanac*. New York: World Publishing Company, 1971.

Thrapp, Dan L. *Encyclopedia of Frontier Biography*. Glendale, CA: Arthur H. Clark Company, 1988.

Traas, Adrian George. *From the Golden Gate to Mexico City: The U.S. Topographical Engineers in the Mexican War, 1846–1848*. Washington, DC: Office of History, Corps of Engineers, US Army, 1993.

Twitchell, Ralph Emerson. *The History of the Military Occupation of the Territory of New Mexico from 1846 to 1851*. Denver: Smith-Brooks Company, 1909.

———. *The Story of the Conquest of Santa Fe, New Mexico, and the Building of Old Fort Marcy, A.D. 1846*. Santa Fe: Historical Society of New Mexico, n.d.

Urwin, Gregory J. W. *The United States Cavalry: An Illustrated History*. Poole, Dorset: UK Blandford Press, 1983.

Utley, Robert M. "Fort Union National Monument–New Mexico." Washington, DC: National Park Service, US Department of the Interior, 1962.

Webb, Dave. *Adventures with the Santa Fe Trail*. Dodge City: Kansas Heritage Center, 1989.

Webb, James Josiah. *Adventures in the Santa Fe Trade, 1844–1847*. Lincoln: University of Nebraska Press, 1995.

Wislizenus, A. *Memoir of a Tour to Northern Mexico, Connected with Col. Doniphan's Expedition*. Washington, DC: 30th Congress, 1st Session, 1848. Senate Miscellaneous Document 26.

Young, Otis E. *The First Military Escort on the Santa Fe Trail, 1829*. Glendale, CA: Arthur H. Clark Company, 1952.

INDEX

Italicized page numbers indicate illustrations.

About the Author

During his four-and-a-half-decade-long writing career, James A. Crutchfield has published nearly seventy books pertaining to United States history and biography. His articles have appeared in magazines, newspapers, and journals across the country, earning multiple awards from *Library Journal*, the Daughters of the American Revolution, the American Association for State and Local History, and Western Writers of America. In 2011, Western Writers of America presented him with the Owen Wister Award for Lifetime Achievement in Western History and Literature. In 2015, Crutchfield was inducted into the Western Writers Hall of Fame housed in the McCracken Research Library at the Buffalo Bill Center of the West in Cody, Wyoming. He lives in Tennessee with his wife, Regena, and their three cats, Zoë, Oliver, and Rufus.